GOD HAS A
WONDERFUL
PLAN FOR YOUR LIFE

The MYTH *of the* MODERN MESSAGE

RAY COMFORT

Living Waters Publications
Bellflower, CA

God Has a Wonderful Plan for Your Life: The Myth of the Modern Message

Living Waters Publications
P.O. Box 1172
Bellflower, CA 90707, USA
www.livingwaters.com

Edited by Lynn Copeland

Cover, page design, and production by Genesis Group

Cover illustration by Gustave Doré, *The Doré Bible Illustrations*, Dover Publications, Inc.; modified by Dale Jackson

Printed in the United States of America

ISBN 978-1-878859-49-5

Unless otherwise indicated, Scripture quotations are from the New King James version, © 1979, 1980, 1982 by Thomas Nelson Inc., Publishers, Nashville, Tennessee.

Scripture quotations designated AMP are from *The Amplified Bible*, © 1958, 1987 by The Lockman Foundation, La Habra, California.

Scripture quotations designated TLB are from *The Living Bible*, © 1971 by Tyndale House Publishers, Inc., Wheaton, Illinois.

Scripture references designated KJV are from the King James Version.

Unless otherwise noted, emphasis within Scriptures and other quotations has been added by the author.

CONTENTS

FOREWORD

O ne cannot fully understand what one is saved to unless one also understands what one is saved from. We are saved from the consequences of our sins, which is hell. Jesus said, "If your hand causes you to stumble, cut it off; it is better for you to enter life crippled, than, having your two hands, to go into hell, into the unquenchable fire" (Mark 9:43). It was with the knowledge of hell that Jesus graciously and lovingly called people to repent of their sins and to trust him as Lord and Savior. He thus began his public ministry proclaiming, "The time is fulfilled, and the kingdom of God is at hand; repent and believe in the gospel" (Mark 1:15).

It is an unfortunate commentary, but we are living in a day when the saving message of Jesus Christ is being lost in our churches. Replacing it is a new set of concerns that are quick to speak of God's love, mercy, and grace, but are slow to take up the implications of His holiness, judgment, and wrath. Being disturbingly silent on the significant issues of sin and judgment to come, much contemporary evangelism is producing a bumper-crop of unregenerate believers.

The erosion of gospel values first came to my attention years ago as a young proclamation evangelist in Connecticut. I was shocked to discover the extent to which the "softer, gentler" vision of God, heralded by the early nineteenth-century Universalist William Ellery Channing, continued to inoculate scores of New England churches to the Christ of the Bible.

Years later, I served Dr. Bill Bright as his theological editor, and was privileged to work with him for seven years. Dr. Bright was well aware of the dangers awaiting the unconverted. Toward the end of his life, his great trepidation for the lost led him to author two additional books: one on the Ten Commandments, and another on the vital subjects of heaven and hell. I was delighted that he was addressing such important topics. The hours I spent editing those two books further solidified in my heart the importance for people to be exposed to the genuine gospel of Jesus Christ.

About the same time, I discovered the evangelism of Ray Comfort. Upon watching his videos, which include Kirk Cameron, it became clear to me that Ray had his finger on the problem. He had made a monumental advance in reclaiming the evangel—all of which he had condensed in an exciting and easy-to-learn approach called "The Way of the Master."

Once I became the pastor of a church, I couldn't wait to implement Ray's materials. So far, I have been privileged to lead our people in several training sessions of "The Way of the Master." The results have been nothing short of remarkable. Not only have trainees developed a greater understanding of the gospel, and a love for the lost, but also we have exposed scores of people to the gospel with the result that many have become Christians. I am also encouraged that some of these new believers have joined our church and are now active participants.

There are many ways to articulate the gospel. But before you begin chapter one of this book, let me ask you to set aside any preconceived thoughts you have about personal evangelism and judge everything you read according to the Scriptures. I believe that you will find here an approach that takes its cue from the very way Jesus of Nazareth called people to the family of God.

JOHN BARBER, PH.D.

Chapter 1

PHENOMENAL GROWTH

We live in exciting times. All around us we are seeing the phenomenal rise of megachurches with congregations in the tens of thousands; pockets of revival have sprung up in the United States and other parts of the world; and we have heard of millions of people in Russia, China, and Africa coming to the Savior.

One evangelist, for example, claims that his worldwide tour has led nearly 1 million people to make decisions for Christ since 2007.[1] A denomination reported nearly 2.5 million decisions for Christ in 2008.[2] One international organization reported over 10 million decisions for Christ in 2009,[3] and another ministry has seen an incredible "45 million documented salvations" worldwide in just six years.[4]

These are indeed exciting times.

Yet, with all the excitement about the growth of the contemporary Church, it seems that many have overlooked a few statistical inconsistencies. Before we look at these, I am reminded of a doctor who said to his patient, "I have some very bad news for you. Your heart is extremely weak, and any bad news could kill you." So, how is your heart? I have some really bad news for you. As you hear it, please be consoled that there is a cure.

An October 2003 survey conducted by the Barna Group found that 45 percent of those who profess to be born-again Christians believed that gambling was morally acceptable. According to the survey, 49 percent believed that "living with someone of the opposite sex without being married" was morally okay. Just under half of those questioned (49 percent) were comfortable with "enjoying sexual thoughts or fantasies about someone," while one-third (33 percent) of those professing to be born again thought that it was okay to kill a baby while it is still in the womb.[5]

In 2001, a survey conducted by the Alan Guttmacher Institute in New York found that "13 percent of abortion patients describe themselves as born-again or evangelical Christians."[6] That is, of all those who actually murdered their own unborn children, nearly one in eight professed faith in Jesus Christ. That is difficult to reconcile with the fact that Christians are supposed to love God and love others as much as they love themselves.

Additionally, according to an article titled "Porn Nation" in *World Magazine*, of the men belonging to the Christian organization Promise Keepers (who make a promise to be "committed to practicing spiritual, moral, ethical, and sexual purity"), 53 percent visit porn sites *every week*.[7] This alarming finding is not confined to the pews. An Internet survey of 6,000 pastors conducted in 2002 found that 30 percent of *pastors* had viewed Internet porn in the last 30 days.[8] This is despite the fact that these men are to be the spiritual leaders of their flocks and their families.

In 2009, the Barna Group found further evidence that all is not well in the contemporary Church:

Among individuals who describe themselves as Christian, for instance, close to half believe that Satan does not exist, one-third contend that Jesus sinned while He was on earth, two-fifths say they do not have a responsibility to share the Christian faith with others, and one-quarter dismiss the idea that the Bible is accurate in all of the principles it teaches.[9]

Think for a moment of the implications of such a theology. Here we have millions of "believers" who supposedly confess that Jesus is Lord, and yet they think He sinned. They either don't know what the Bible teaches about the Son of God or they believe it is inaccurate when it says that Jesus "knew no sin" (2 Corinthians 5:21), that He was "in all points tempted as we are, yet without sin" (Hebrews 4:15), and that He "committed no sin, nor was deceit found in His mouth" (1 Peter 2:22). Furthermore, if Jesus sinned, it would mean that He was not the spotless Lamb of God the Scriptures say He was (see 1 Peter 1:19); that His sacrifice was not perfect; and that when God accepted Jesus' death as an atonement for our sins, He sanctioned a "contaminated payment" and is therefore corrupt by nature. Sadly, the multitudes who profess faith in Jesus, yet deny His sinless perfection, appear to be strangers to true regeneration. The Jesus they believe in isn't capable of saving anyone.

In addition, 41 percent of self-proclaimed Christians believe that "the Bible, the Koran and the Book of Mormon are all different expressions of the same spiritual truths"[10]—despite the books' vastly contradictory teachings on truth, salvation, and the nature of God. And only 46 percent of born-again adults believe in the existence of absolute moral truth.[11] So that means the other 54 percent don't think that God has moral absolutes, which perhaps explains why so many live their lives as though there is no moral accountability at all.

Pollster George Barna, in observing these troubling trends, noted, "Although most Americans consider themselves to be Christian and say they know the content of the Bible, less than one out of ten Americans demonstrate such knowledge through their actions."[12] With over 173 million Christians in the U.S.,[13] there are tens of millions who say that they love God and yet they are liars, thieves, fornicators, adulterers, and child-murderers. Paul's warning to Titus seems to be true of much of the modern Church: "They profess to know God, but in works they deny Him" (Titus 1:16). Neither their beliefs nor their behavior aligns with biblical Christianity.

Leaving in Droves

Sadly, young people today are exhibiting the same theological confusion as the preceding generation. Despite 8 out of 10 teens describing themselves as Christian, 61 percent believe a place in Heaven can be *earned* through good works; 63 percent believe Muslims, Buddhists, Christians, Jews, and all other people pray to the same God; and 58 percent believe all religious faiths teach equally valid truths.[14]

As with adults, the behavior of youth who describe themselves as Christian is virtually indistinguishable from that of non-Christians. An "Ethics of American Youth Survey" found that in the prior 12 months 74 percent of *Christian* teens cheated on a test, 93 percent lied to a parent, and 63 percent physically hurt someone when angered.[15] The Barna Group also found that teens who profess to be born again and attend church regularly were just as likely as secular teens to engage in Internet theft of music and to illegally copy CDs (77 percent to 81 percent, respectively).[16]

In a joint statement, youth specialists Josh McDowell and Ron Luce made a sobering announcement: "Incredible as it may seem, 'accepting Christ' and making a profession of faith makes little to no difference in a young person's attitudes and behaviors. The majority of our churched young people are adopting 'a Christianity' but it is not true Christianity." While this is a shocking admission, McDowell and Luce are not alone in their conclusion. Ninety-eight percent of youth ministers and pastors McDowell surveyed agree with that assessment.[17]

As with adults, the behavior of youth who describe themselves as Christian is virtually indistinguishable from that of non-Christians.

If that isn't alarming enough, another trend is helping to further paint a bleak picture of the state of the American Church. In researching families in the U.S., the Southern Baptist Council on Family Life discovered a gut-wrenching statistic: "88 percent of the children raised in evangelical homes leave church at the age of 18, never to return."[18] This mass exodus is seen not just among Southern Baptist churches, but across denominational lines.[19]

In an interview on a popular national radio program, a Christian youth leader spoke with great concern about how young people were "leaving the church in droves." He had taken a survey to find out why these teenagers were turning their backs on God, and he cited the number one reason as "a lack of opportunity in the church"—implying that the Church should get its act together and give young people more opportunities. Ask any pastor if there are opportunities to serve within his church, and he will no doubt tell you of the lack of people willing to teach Sunday school, visit the sick and the elderly, go out with the evangelism team, clean the church building, etc.

Perhaps there is another reason that young people are leaving the Church in droves. As these statistics show, there are many today who name the name of Christ, but who have failed to "depart from iniquity [lawlessness]" (2 Timothy 2:19). They are false converts who have "asked Jesus into their hearts," yet they remain unconverted because they have never truly repented.

I cannot put into words the heartbreak of seeing so many spurious converts who have left the Church, and the multitudes of false converts who stay within the Church. Prolific author and pastor A. W. Tozer writes,

> It is my opinion that tens of thousands of people, if not millions, have been brought into some kind of religious experience by accepting Christ, and they have not been saved.

Tozer is not alone in his conclusion. The late pastor D. James Kennedy, of Coral Ridge Ministries, made a similar observation:

> The vast majority of people who are members of churches in America today are not Christians. I say that without the slightest fear of contradiction. I base it on empirical evidence of twenty-four years of examining thousands of people.

Many of us, if asked which U.S. denomination is most evangelistic, would point to the Southern Baptists. But in trying to determine why there is so much "evangelistic apathy" in their churches, Thom Rainer, president and CEO of LifeWay Christian Resources, found that the cause could be their "many unregenerate members." Rainer stated, "If our research approximates eternal realities, nearly one-half of all church members may not be Christians."[20]

How could this tragic situation have happened? How could vast numbers of people have been led to believe that they are Christians when they are not? If you have struggled to understand why a loved one who made a "decision for Christ" has no desire for the things of God, or why so many church members show little to no evidence for their faith, there is an explanation. And there is something you can do to change the situation.

The Parabolic Key

Though the idea of false conversions may be new to us, the problem of false converts has existed since the beginning of the Church and it is actually a topic Jesus spoke often about. For example, in Mark 4:3–8, Jesus taught the crowd the well-known parable of the sower:

> "Listen! Behold, a sower went out to sow. And it happened, as he sowed, that some seed fell by the wayside; and the birds of the air came and devoured it. Some fell on stony ground, where it did not have much earth; and immediately it sprang up because it had no depth of earth. But when the sun was up it was scorched, and because it had no root it withered away. And some seed fell among thorns; and the thorns grew up and choked it, and it yielded no crop.

But other seed fell on good ground and yielded a crop that sprang up, increased and produced: some thirtyfold, some sixty, and some a hundred."

When Jesus told His disciples the parable of the sower, they did not understand what it meant. When they asked Him about it later, He said, "Do you not understand this parable? How then will you understand all the parables?" (Mark 4:13). In other words, if they could comprehend the parable of the sower, they would hold the key to unlocking the mysteries of all the other parables.

If there is one message that comes from the parable about the stony ground, the thorny ground, and the good ground, it is this: When the gospel is preached, there will be true and false conversions.

Judas Iscariot, for example, was a false convert. He was a hypocrite—a pretender—whose desire (it seems) for riches and power choked out his affection for Christ. In terms of the parable, we would say that he was a thorny-ground hearer, in whom "the cares of this world, the deceitfulness of riches, and the desires for other things entering in choke the word, and it becomes unfruitful" (Mark 4:19).

Judas had no idea who Jesus really was. When a woman anointed Jesus with an expensive ointment in an act of sacrificial worship, Judas complained that the ointment should have been sold and the money given to the poor (see John 12:3–6). In his estimation, Jesus of Nazareth wasn't worth such extravagance—He was worth only about thirty pieces of silver. Moreover, the Bible tells us that Judas was lying when he said that he cared for the poor. He was actually a thief who so lacked a healthy fear of God that he was stealing money from the collection bag (see John 12:6). Nevertheless, to all outward appearances, Judas was a follower and disciple of Christ.

If one grasps the principle that true and false converts will be alongside each other in the Church, then the other parables about the kingdom of God also make sense: the wheat and tares (Matthew 13:24–30), the good fish and the bad fish (Matthew 13:47–50), the wise virgins and the foolish virgins (Matthew 25:1–13), and the sheep and goats (Matthew 25:31–46). Take, for example, the parable of the dragnet:

> "Again, the kingdom of heaven is like a dragnet that was cast into the sea and gathered some of every kind, which, when it was full, they drew to shore; and they sat down and gathered the good into vessels, but threw the bad away. So it will be at the end of the age. The angels will come forth, separate the wicked from among the just, and cast them into the furnace of fire. There will be wailing and gnashing of teeth." (Matthew 13:47–50)

Notice that the good fish and the bad fish were in the net together. Notice also that unbelievers are not caught in the dragnet of the kingdom of Heaven; they remain in the world. The "fish" that are caught are those who hear and respond to the gospel—the evangelistic "catch." They remain together, the true and the false, until the Day of Judgment.

In Matthew 7:21–23, possibly the most frightening passage in Scripture, Jesus spoke of *many* who would consider themselves Christians and yet not be saved. Jesus warned, "Not everyone who says to Me, 'Lord, Lord,' shall enter the kingdom of heaven... Many will say to Me in that day, 'Lord, Lord, have we not prophesied in Your name, cast out demons in Your name, and done many wonders in Your name?' And then I will declare to them, 'I never knew you; depart from Me, you who practice lawlessness.'"

Look at how seemingly spiritual people can be and still not make it to Heaven:

- They called Jesus "Lord."

- They prophesied in His name.

- They cast out demons.

- They did many "wonders" in His name.

These people are more spiritual than most of us, and yet they will be rejected by the One they call "Lord." False converts *do* have a measure of spirituality. Judas certainly did. He had apparently convinced the other disciples that he truly cared for the poor. And he seemed so trustworthy that he was the one who looked after the finances. When Jesus said, "One of you will betray Me," the disciples didn't point the finger at Judas; instead, they suspected themselves, saying, "Lord, is it I?" That's why it's not surprising that so few within the Church today would suspect that we are surrounded by those who fall into the "Judas" category.

I would like to caution you at this point: In case you think the problem of false converts affects only those "other churches," let me say that statistics show otherwise. As we will see in a subsequent chapter, 80–90 percent of those making decisions for Christ—whether through large crusades or local church efforts—will fall away. We will explore numerous statistics later, but here is one example:

In the March/April 1993 issue of *American Horizon*, a major U.S. denomination disclosed that in 1991, 11,500 churches had obtained 294,784 decisions for Christ. Unfortunately, they could find only 14,337 in fellowship. This means that, despite the usual intense follow-up, they could not account for approximately 280,000 (95 percent) of their "converts."

For a more personal example, consider one individual's account following a crusade:

> Our church, which participated at every stage, received about 25 names for follow-up. These were mostly people in our area who did not identify with a church. We were instructed that many of these decisions might be fuzzy about what happened at the crusade and we should make sure they really understood the gospel. But, we had cold receptions and not even enough interest to even begin the recommended Bible study class for new believers. To my knowledge none of those twenty-five even visited our church after several contacts and pastoral visits.[21]

With the vast majority of "converts" falling away, could some of those whom you have led to the Lord be among the "many" who will hear Jesus say, "Depart from Me"? As much as any of us would be horrified to think we are creating "Judases," it is likely that you too may be leading people into false conversions through your evangelism efforts. The Body of Christ is not as healthy as we might like to believe—and the problem is systemic. *Something* is radically wrong. Before we look at the remedy, however, we must consider the cause. For the sake of the lost, please keep reading.

Chapter 2

THE WAY OUT OF PROBLEMS?

In light of the alarming statistics cited in the previous chapter, few would deny that the Church as a whole has fallen short of the powerful, disciplined, sanctified Church seen in the Book of Acts. This is a result of the enemy subtly diverting our attention away from our core message. Instead of preaching the Good News that sinners can be made righteous in Christ and escape the wrath to come, we have settled for a "gospel" that implies that God's primary purpose in saving us is to unfold a "wonderful plan" for our lives: to solve our problems, make us happy in Christ, and rescue us from the hassles of this life.

You may know someone who responded to the "God has a wonderful plan" message and who seems to be doing just fine. If you think that justifies the method, let me share a perspective you may not have considered.

Imagine that someone invented a parachute that was 100 percent trustworthy; the chute opened every time, without exception, and got the wearer safely to the ground. The key was to diligently follow the manufacturer's instructions. Now imagine that the packers began to ignore the instructions and use a new "fast-and-easy" method of folding that greatly increased production. Everyone rejoiced that so much time and effort could now be saved.

As time passed, however, it became evident that something was radically wrong. They discovered that nine out of every ten people who jumped with the "fast-folded" parachutes fell to their deaths!

What would you say to someone who ignored the 90 percent of dead, mangled bodies on the ground, and pointed to the 10 percent "success" rate for justification of their methods? The "God has a wonderful plan" method is easy—but it is also devastating. As we will see, we have tampered with the instructions on how to reach the lost, with dire eternal consequences.

A Better Life

One of America's largest Christian publishers produces a full-color tract that epitomizes the promise of a hassle-free life. Titled "Is There Any Way Out?", it reads:

> Everyone is looking for a way out of their problems … There's no easy way out. You won't get respect by joining a gang. You won't find love in the backseat of a car. You'll never find success by dropping out of school. And the chances are about one million to one that you'll win the lottery. If you're *really* serious about making your life better, then try God's way. God gets right to the source of most of our problems: sin.

It may sound admirable—and even biblical to some —to imply to sinners that Christianity promises to solve their problems and make their lives better, but it's just not true.

It seems that some are so entrenched in the "wonderful plan" message that they don't equate *real* life with the message they preach. Based on many years of itinerant ministry, I know it is no exaggeration to say that the following scenario is commonplace in many pulpits each Sunday morning:

> God has a wonderful plan for your life. He wants to give you true happiness and to fill the God-shaped hole in your heart that you've been trying to fill with sex, drugs, alcohol, and money. Jesus said that He came to give you life, and give it "more abundantly." So come forward now and give your life to Jesus, so that you can experience this wonderful new life in Christ.
>
> While they are coming, let's pray for the Smiths, who lost their two children in a car accident this week. Brother Jones has been diagnosed with cancer. Remember to uphold the whole family. His wife had another miscarriage on Tuesday, and both of their other children are chronic asthmatics. Sister Bryant fell and broke her hip. She's such a dear saint—she's had trial after trial in her life, especially since the death of her husband, Ernie. Elder Chambers lost his job this week. That will make things difficult for the Chambers family, especially with his upcoming triple-bypass operation. Sister Lancing died of kidney failure on Monday night. Keep the Lancing family in prayer, because it's their third tragedy this year.
>
> How many of you this morning need prayer for sickness or have problems with depression? That many? You had better stay in your seats, and we will have a corporate prayer.

It may sound admirable—even biblical—to imply to sinners that Christianity promises to solve their problems and make their lives better, but it's just not true.

This makes no sense. The preacher promises a bed of roses for those who come to Christ, but those who are in Christ are evidently sitting on a painful bed of thorns. He assures a smooth flight, but those who are already on board are suffering terrible turbulence—and no one seems to notice the paradox.

Let me tell you about a few of my Christian friends who live in the real world. One went with his wife to a meeting. Their teenage son drove there alone. On the way home, my friend came across an accident, so he stopped to help. When he looked in the vehicle, he saw his beloved teenage son, dead—impaled on the steering wheel.

The senior pastor of a church where I was on staff was roused from his bed at three o'clock one morning to counsel a man who had come to his door and was waiting in the living room. As the pastor stepped into the room, the man began to slash him with a machete. The pastor almost died, and was irrevocably scarred both physically and mentally, so much so that he was unable to minister and required twenty-four-hour care.

Another pastor friend learned that his wife had multiple sclerosis. Her crippling disease left him as the only one in the family able to take care of their three young boys. Then he was diagnosed with cancer. His wife died after struggling with her disease for many years.

One of my friends, a graphic artist, married a woman whose Christian husband had died of cancer, leaving her to rear five kids. The marriage seemed fine until she ran off with another man. She left my friend with the one child that was his. Some time after that, someone broke into his home and beat him to a pulp. He had to be rushed to the emergency room for treatment.

On June 19, 2000, five trainees with New Tribes Mission pitched a tent during a violent storm in Mississippi. Jenny Knapp, an attractive twenty-year-old, noticed that rain was causing the roof to cave in, so she lifted the tent pole to raise the height of the roof. Suddenly, a bolt of lightning struck the pole and tore through her body, giving her second-degree burns on her face, arm, and back. Her friends resuscitated her lifeless body and rushed her to the hospital where she was placed in the intensive care unit. The young missionary recovered, but she is terribly scarred and partially blind. It is a sad fact of life, but in the real world, lightning strikes the just and the unjust. At least one church I know of may have noticed the paradox. They were called "The Happy Church," but recently decided, for some reason, to change their name.

The Wonderfulness of Martyrdom

If we still want to cling to the message that "God has a wonderful plan for your life," we had better hide *Foxe's Book of Martyrs* from the eyes of non-Christians. Speaking of martyrdom, have you ever pondered what it would be like to be huddling together with your family in a Roman arena as hungry and ferocious lions rush in? Have you ever considered what it would be like to be eaten by lions? I have. My fertile imagination runs wild. What do you give the lion to eat first—your arm? How long would you remain conscious as he gnawed on it?

Can you imagine the feelings you would have if you had led your loved ones in a "sinner's prayer" using the "wonderful plan" hook? Suppose you had read to them from a booklet by a well-known and respected man of God in which he writes, "Everyone is seeking happiness.

Why, then, are more people not experiencing this happiness? According to the Bible, true happiness can be found only through God's way."

What would you tell your beloved family as you looked into their terrified eyes? How could you reconcile the words "wonderful" and "happiness" with having the fierce teeth of a lion rip you apart, limb from limb?

These are terrible thoughts, but they are not merely my fantasies. Multitudes of martyrs have suffered unspeakable torture for the cause of Christ. It should not have been a surprise to the early Church when persecution hit them. Jesus warned them that they may have to give their lives for His name's sake. He even said, "Brother will deliver up brother to death, and a father his child; and children will rise up against parents and cause them to be put to death. And you will be hated by all for My name's sake" (Matthew 10:21,22).

Church tradition tells us the fate of several apostles and early evangelists:

Philip: Crucified, Phrygia, A.D. 54

Matthew: Beheaded, Ethiopia, A.D. 60

Barnabas: Burned to death, Cyprus, A.D. 64

Mark: Dragged to death, Alexandria, A.D. 64

James (the Less): Clubbed to death, Jerusalem, A.D. 66

Paul: Beheaded, Rome, A.D. 66

Peter: Crucified, Rome, A.D. 69

Andrew: Crucified, Achaia, A.D. 70

Thomas: Speared to death, Calamina, A.D. 70

Luke: Hanged, Athens, A.D. 93

Persecution has always been the portion of the godly. According to Scripture:

> Others were tortured . . . Still others had trial of mockings and scourgings, yes, and of chains and imprisonment. They were stoned, they were sawn in two, were tempted, were slain with the sword. They wandered about in sheepskins and goatskins, being destitute, afflicted, tormented—of whom the world was not worthy. They wandered in deserts and mountains, in dens and caves of the earth. (Hebrews 11:35–38)

Perhaps some would argue that the Christian life is a wonderful plan because "all things work together for good to those who love God" (Romans 8:28). That fact is wonderful in the truest sense of the word. No matter what happens to us as Christians, we can rejoice because of that promise. But the promise does not guarantee that our lives will be without suffering and trial and pain.

In 1413, John Hus was summoned to appear before the Roman Church council in Constance. When he was thrown into a prison for nineteen months awaiting trial for his faith and then sentenced to death, he no doubt knew that God would work things out for his good. When he was burned alive at the stake and his charred, lifeless body fell among the ashes, the wonderful promise that God would work out for his good such an unspeakable horror remained unwavering.

On November 9, 2006, three Christian teenagers were beheaded by Indonesian militants. Their severed heads were dumped in plastic bags in their village, along with a handwritten note threatening more such attacks. If these girls loved God and were called according to His purpose, they too could claim this incredible promise.

In Malatya, Turkey, when three Christian men working in a Bible publishing office were accosted by Muslims on April 18, 2007, they no doubt knew that God would work all things together for good. As their hands and feet were bound, they were tortured with butcher knives, and finally their throats were cut, the promise remained steadfast.

According to Gordon-Conwell Theological Seminary, worldwide an average of 171,000 Christians *annually* are martyred for their faith.[22] The promise of Romans 8:28 is also true for each and every one of these children of God.

Examine the Book of Acts and see if you can find any of the disciples telling sinners either that God loved them or that He had a wonderful plan for their lives.

If indeed our Creator works all things out for good—if He brings ultimate good out of every agony suffered by His children—why then shouldn't we use that truth as bait when fishing for men? For one thing, the phrase "wonderful plan" has *positive* connotations; it doesn't typically evoke negative images of machetes, hatred, persecution, beatings, and martyrdom. If non-Christians respond to the gospel message only to improve their lives, they will be disillusioned when persecution comes, and they may fall away from the faith. This is because many respond experimentally, simply to see if the "wonderful life" is as good as Christians say it is.

But the most important reason not to use the "wonderful plan" message is that it isn't biblical to do so. Examine the Book of Acts and see if you can find any of the disciples telling sinners either that God loved them or that He had a wonderful plan for their lives.[23] If there is no precedent for this approach in Scripture, the question isn't "Why *not* use it?" but "Why even consider it in the first place?" Why would we not carefully follow the pattern given for us in Scripture, by the Master Evangelist, especially on something as crucial as the salvation of eternal souls?

Instead, we see that the disciples confronted their hearers as guilty criminals—enemies of God who desperately needed righteousness, not to be told that they could enhance their lives with God's wonderful plan.

Jesus didn't shield the newly converted Saul of Tarsus from what was in store for him as a Christian. Instead, Jesus said that He would "show him *how many things he must suffer* for My name's sake" (Acts 9:16). Stephen was cruelly stoned to death for his faith. James, who told his brethren to "count it all joy when you fall into various trials" (James 1:2), was murdered with a sword. John the Baptist also felt the sharp steel of persecution. Down through the ages, Christians have been hated, persecuted, thrown to lions, beheaded, and—like John Hus—even burned at the stake for the sake of the gospel.

All this is consistent with Scriptures admonishing us to count the cost of following Jesus: "If they persecuted Me, they will also persecute you" (John 15:20); "In the world you will have tribulation" (John 16:33); "We must through many tribulations enter the kingdom of God" (Acts 14:22); and countless others. The promise of the gospel has never been one of an enhanced life on earth. During our brief sojourn here we are to forsake all that we have, deny ourselves, and take up the cross daily; we will be hated for His name's sake, and if we live a godly life, we shall suffer persecution (see 2 Timothy 3:12). Jesus warned those who followed Him that the time would come when people would murder them, and think they were doing God a favor by spilling their blood (see John 16:2).

In light of the fact that Christians in numerous countries yet today are deprived of their possessions, harassed, imprisoned, or killed for their faith, perhaps the message that "God has a wonderful plan for your life" applies only to the United States. One might have offered that argument until the shooting deaths of Christians in America in recent years. Christians were targeted in the Columbine High School massacre, and in a December 2007 shooting in Colorado, where a gunman attacked a missionary training center and then hours later a church, killing four people and wounding five others.[24]

Not So Wonderful

If you still want to hold on to the modern approach to evangelism, let me try one other thought that should convince you that the "wonderful plan" message is erroneous and misleading.

Imagine that you have been supernaturally taken back to September 10, 2001. You have been asked to address the people who work in Tower One of the World Trade Center. Your topic is "The Benefits of the Christian Life." What an incredible opportunity you have to reach the lost!

You look at the vast sea of faces in front of you. There are mothers and fathers, husbands and wives, sons and daughters. Many have already made retirement plans. Others have made plans to be with their families for Christmas. Just like you, they have hopes, dreams, and fears.

What are you going to say to these people? Are you going to tell them what a wonderful plan God has for them? How could you? You know that within twenty-four hours many of your hearers will die in unspeakably horrible ways. In an instant, some will become human torches as jet fuel saturates them and their bodies ignite and burn to ashes. Others will be terribly suffocated in a huge ball of fiery, poisonous gases as their burning lungs gasp for breath. Rather than face the horror of dying in the flames, some will jump more than one hundred stories in inconceivable terror to their deaths on the unforgiving sidewalks of New York City. Those who manage to stay alive on the upper floors will eventually come crashing down, along with the earthshaking weight of twisted metal and concrete, their bodies so horribly mangled and ripped apart that they will be unidentifiable. Many others, working on the lower floors, will be crushed like helpless spiders as the building collapses.

The lost don't equate the promise of a "wonderful plan for your life" with eternity. They understandably think of the here and now.

Again, what will you tell them? Can you in good conscience say, "God has a wonderful plan for your life"?

You may be thinking, *Hold on. God does have a wonderful plan for their lives—for their eternity.* Your thought is that if they give their lives to Christ, they will go to Heaven after they have been burned to death or smashed on the sidewalk. But the lost don't equate the promise of a "wonderful plan for your *life*" with eternity. They understandably think of the here and now.

I would say that I could never tell those people that God has a wonderful plan for their lives (and I trust you feel the same). The reality is that every 24 hours, 150,000 people around the world die and enter eternity—most without the Savior. According to the World Health Organization, cancer dragged 7.9 million victims to their graves in 2007,[25] and heart disease killed 7.2 million.[26] Each year 1.27 million people die in traffic accidents.[27] Worldwide annual deaths from the flu are estimated to be between 250,000 and 500,000,[28] and in the U.S. alone, each year around 100,000 are helped out of here through hospital-related infections.[29] If dirty hospitals don't kill people, incompetence may—between 40,000 and 100,000 people die annually due to doctors' mistakes.[30]

We never know when death will seize upon someone. So, if that popular message is not appropriate for the people who worked in the World Trade Center—or for those with terminal diseases, those who will soon be killed through accidents or violence, those who will face suffering in this life, and so on—how then can it be the biblical gospel? The gospel message recorded in Scripture transcends time, place, and circumstances. It is the same message for *all* mankind throughout history.

Perhaps you are thinking, *This guy is destroying my gospel presentation. Now what am I going to tell non-Christians? What would bring someone to the Savior if not the promise of a wonderful new life in Christ?* If that is your view, please be patient with me. We will answer these questions in a subsequent chapter. But before looking at the biblical approach to the gospel, we will first consider some additional concerns with using the "wonderful plan" message.

Chapter 3

THE HAPPINESS DILEMMA

A s we have seen, telling people that God has a wonderful plan for their lives isn't being honest about the realities of life. And here is the double tragedy. When the Church declares the message that "Jesus solves problems" or "Jesus provides happiness," it restricts the field of evangelistic endeavor to those in society who will be interested—those who are unhappy and caught up in their problems.

These "problem" people are not given the message of sin, righteousness, and judgment with the command to repent and flee from the wrath to come. Instead, they are told that Jesus is the answer to their alcohol, drug, marriage, personal, or financial problems, and that He is the one who can fill the God-shaped hole in their lives. Many, therefore, come only to have their problems solved.

However, if they do not repent of their sin (because they haven't been told to), they will have a false conversion (see Mark 4:16,17) and they will not become new creatures in Christ. Though they may call Jesus "Lord," they will continue to "practice lawlessness" (see Matthew 7:23). Consequently, they will bring their sins and their problems into the local church, which has the following unfortunate effects:

- Wearing out the pastors. Instead of being able to give themselves fully to feeding the flock of God in the capacity of shepherd, pastors find themselves forever counseling those who are only hearers of the Word and not doers.

- Tying up the laborers (who are already few in number) by having them spend their precious time propping people up, when what these "problem" people really need is repentance.

- Hindering the furtherance of the gospel. Probably one of the biggest stumbling blocks for unbelievers is what they see as rampant hypocrisy within the Church.

In a publication titled *What Do You Want from Life?*, the conclusion is drawn that we all want to be happy. Despite the list of things cited—sex, money, friends, fame, love, and so on—the question is posed: Can we be *truly* and continually happy? The answer provided is, of course, that knowing Jesus produces "ultra happiness ... your happiest moment magnified a million times over."

Not many would see that there is anything wrong with this publication. However, the call of the gospel is universal and is not confined to the unhappy, "hurting" world, as it is so often promoted. The gospel is a promise of *righteousness*, not a promise of happiness, and it therefore may also be offered to those who are enjoying the "pleasures of sin for a season." Prior to my conversion, I was very happy, satisfied, thankful, and joyful. At the age of twenty I was a successful businessman with my own house, a beautiful wife, a car, money, and, being self-employed, the freedom to enjoy it all. I was loving life and living it to the fullest. *Therefore, I was not a candidate for the modern gospel.* I wasn't hurting in the slightest. I had a wonderful life without Jesus. However, when I was confronted with the biblical gospel and understood that "riches do not profit in the day of wrath, but *righteousness* delivers from death" (Proverbs 11:4), I saw my need for the Savior.

Let me repeat: Because of the erroneous belief that the chief end of the gospel is man's happiness on earth rather than righteousness, many fail to see its God-given intention. They think the gospel is only for those who lack money, those who are brokenhearted by life's difficulties, those who are the problem people in society. The belief is further perpetuated through popular worship choruses that have splendid melodies, but carry this message: "Heartaches, broken people, ruined lives are why You died on Calvary." How often do we therefore neglect to share the gospel with those whose lives are going well, because we know they won't be interested in the "wonderful plan" message? We may wait for a crisis to come their way—and in fact, secretly hope that it does—so their "heartaches" will then make them receptive to our offer of a better life.

Who Is the Gospel For?

We limit our evangelistic outreaches when we bill them as "taking the Good News to the hurting and the needy." Let me further illustrate this common misunderstanding by quoting from another modern publication:

> You will desire to be where the Lord is. And He spends His time with those who hurt. At the beginning of His ministry, Jesus quoted Isaiah to describe

the work He was called to do: "The Spirit of the Lord is upon Me, because He has anointed Me to preach the gospel to the poor; He has sent Me to heal the brokenhearted, to proclaim liberty to the captives, and recovery of sight to the blind, to set at liberty those who are oppressed; to proclaim the acceptable year of the Lord" (Luke 4:18,19)...Thus the more you go after God, the deeper you will move into a world filled with hurting people.

I am in no way questioning the sincerity of the author, but I believe he perpetuates a common misunderstanding of what Jesus intended to communicate when he quoted from Isaiah 61:1,2. We live in a "therapeutic" culture that places a high value on feeling good, self-esteem, and self-actualization. Consequently, when we see words like "poor," "brokenhearted," and "oppressed," we think of people who are beset by life's circumstances, whether it's poverty, divorce, addiction, or disease. Jesus, however, is speaking primarily in *spiritual* terms.

From Luke 4:18,19, here is Jesus' summation of who the gospel is for:

- The poor

- The brokenhearted

- The captives

- The blind

- The oppressed

When Jesus speaks of the *poor*, He is not necessarily referring to those who lack financial resources. Instead, He is referring to the "poor in spirit" (Matthew 5:3)—those who are meek, humble, lowly. These are the blessed ones to whom the kingdom of God belongs: those who know that they are destitute of righteousness. In his commentary on Luke 4:14–30, Matthew Henry writes:

> Observe... to *whom* He was to preach: to the *poor*; to those that were *poor in the world*; whom the Jewish doctors disdained to undertake the teaching of and spoke of with contempt; to those that were *poor in spirit*, to the meek and humble, and to those that were truly sorrowful for sin.[31] (emphasis in the original)

When Jesus speaks of the *brokenhearted*, He doesn't mean those unhappy people whose hearts are aching because they have been jilted by a sweetheart, but those who, like Peter and Isaiah, are contrite and sorrowing for their sin. In David's great prayer of confession, he realized that the sacrifices God desires are "a broken spirit, a broken and a contrite heart" (Psalm 51:17). In the words of Matthew Henry, "[Christ] was sent to heal the brokenhearted,... to give peace to those that were troubled and humbled for sins,... and to bring them to rest who were weary and heavy-laden, under the burden of guilt and corruption."[32]

The *captives* are those "taken captive by [the devil] to do his will" (2 Timothy 2:26).

The *blind* are those whom "the god of this age has blinded... [to] the light of the gospel of the glory of Christ" (2 Corinthians 4:4).

The *oppressed* are those who are "oppressed by the devil" (Acts 10:38).

In other words, Jesus came to preach the Good News of God's forgiveness to those who recognize their spiritual poverty and are broken by the realization that they have sinned against a just and holy God. That isn't to say that Jesus did not minister to those who were beset by life's circumstances—but His message was not only for those people, and the freedom He offered was not freedom from the hardships of life. Again, the gospel is not confined to the hurting people with ruined lives and heartaches. Both hurting *and* happy people need to be shown their sinful state before God so they will seek after the righteousness that is in Christ.

One atheist, understandably confused by the life-enhancement message, observed: "At one church I visited, some people were asked to write down how they felt before and after becoming Christian. They said things like 'dark and light,' 'lonely and befriended,' which got me wondering: Was being down or lonely or desperate a prerequisite to finding God? Did these people think that others who had not yet found God were lost, scared or miserable? Do I have to go through some sort of trauma or crisis before finding some ultimate meaning?"[33]

The Competition

Another dilemma with the life-enhancement message is this: If you search the Internet using the keywords "true happiness," you will find many websites offering Jesus as a solution. However, the idea that "Jesus gives true happiness" has some competition. There are more than 100,000,000 other results to the keywords "true happiness," many of which refer to self-help strategies, such as that proposed by author Martin E. P. Seligman in *Authentic Happiness: Using the New Positive Psychology to Realize Your Potential for Lasting Fulfillment.*

The Jehovah's Witnesses believe they have the answer for happiness. Their *Watchtower* magazine states, "Through a study of the Bible, you can find true happiness despite your problems...Jehovah's Witnesses will be pleased to show you the Scriptural answers that you need to know if you are to be truly happy."[34]

Buddhism likewise claims to be the path to true happiness, as the *Basic Buddhism Guide* assures us: "Buddhism explains a purpose to life, it explains apparent injustice and inequality around the world, and it provides a code of practice or way of life that leads to true happiness."[35]

Both hurting and happy people need to be shown their sinful state before God so they will seek after the righteousness in Christ.

Hinduism offers the same thing: "Without remembering the name of God, even the sovereign King of the world, would be unhappy...By dwelling on the Name of God, he can obtain true happiness. Hence, realization of God is the key that unlocks the doors to unending happiness, eternal peace of mind and unimaginable bliss."[36]

So does Islam. In a lecture delivered in Washington, Maulana Shah Muhammad Abdul Aleem Siddiqui al Qaderi expounded on "The Quest for True Happiness." He said, "Here I shall state some basic facts, and the principles pertaining thereto, so that if anyone practices them, he or she may attain peace of mind, comfort of the soul and true happiness."[37]

In December 2007, a Gallup poll asked Americans how satisfied they were with their personal lives. Fifty-two percent responded that they were "very happy," and another 40 percent said that they were "fairly happy."[38] So the modern gospel has some stiff competition—the vast majority of people in the United States are already enjoying a wonderful plan for their lives, and they are quite happy as they are. For any who do feel something is missing and look to religion for happiness, they will find a smorgasbord of choices all offering to improve their life on earth.

If only Jesus gives *true* happiness, as the modern gospel message maintains, then it follows that the happiness the world gives must be false—or at the very least, shallow. Consequently, the Christian sees his job as one of unmasking the world's promise of happiness and contrasting it with the true and lasting happiness that Jesus gives. From there arises the "Jesus is better than beer" mentality. This is demeaning to the name of Jesus, and completely unnecessary. There is no contest between Jesus and beer, because happiness isn't the issue.

The Abundant Life

Still, the question may arise, why not use the fact that Jesus said He had come to bring us an abundant life (John 10:10) to draw unregenerate sinners to the Savior? True, the Christian life is full. Consider the full life of Paul. Read 2 Corinthians 11:23–28 and see if you think he was bored while being stoned (once), shipwrecked (three times), beaten (three times), and whipped (five times). His life *was* full. There were also times when he wasn't happy. In fact, at one point he was in such despair that he wanted to die (see 2 Corinthians 1:8).

The apostle gives the carnal-minded Corinthians a glimpse of the abundant life. He told them that he had been condemned to death. He was hungry and thirsty. He lacked clothing. He was beaten and had nowhere to live. He was reviled, persecuted, slandered, and treated as the filth of the world. What a terrible, uninviting path Paul walked down. If happiness were the goal, one would think that he would put up a sign saying "Don't enter here." However, he did the opposite. He told the Corinthians to imitate him (see 1 Corinthians 4:9–16). He considered that the sufferings of this life are not worthy to be compared to life in eternity (see Romans 8:18).

Like Jesus, the apostle Paul taught that the Christian life is one of self-denial—that we are to crucify the flesh, daily take up the cross, deny ourselves, and follow Jesus. However, the "wonderful plan" message, with its promise of earthly happiness, appeals solely to the hearer's selfishness. By offering a problem-free life, it encourages continued love of self rather than God, and paints Him as a divine butler.

Where Is God's Love?

If we cannot give sinners the message that God has a wonderful plan for their lives, how do we tell them about God's love? As we have seen, the apostle Paul faced countless trials and tribulations, was mocked and hated, imprisoned for years, and finally martyred. What did he look to for assurance of God's love for him?

He did not look to his lifestyle, because to the untrained eye, it did not exactly speak of God's caring hand for him. His "abundant" life was certainly full, but it was not full of what we might expect if God loved him.

Picture Paul, lying half-naked on a cold dungeon floor, chained to hardened Roman guards. You look at his bloody back and his bruised, swollen face and you say, "Paul, you've been beaten again. Where are your friends? Demas and the others have forsaken you. Where is your expensive chariot and your successful building program? Where is the evidence of God's blessing, Paul? What's that? What did you say? Did I hear you mumble through swollen lips that God loves you?"

Now picture Paul slowly lifting his head. His blackened, bruised eyes look deeply into yours. They sparkle as he says two words: "The cross!" He painfully reaches into his blood-soaked tunic and carefully pulls out a letter he had been writing. His trembling and bloodstained finger points to one sentence. You strain your eyes in the dim light and read, "I have been crucified with Christ; it is no longer I who live, but Christ lives in me; and the life which I now live in the flesh I live by faith in the Son of God, *who loved me and gave Himself for me*" (Galatians 2:20).

Those who look to the cross as a token of God's love will never doubt His steadfast devotion to them, regardless of their circumstances.

Christ's sacrifice was the source of Paul's joy and thus his strength: "God forbid that I should boast except in the cross of our Lord Jesus Christ" (Galatians 6:14). If you study the New Testament you will see that God's love is almost always given in direct correlation to the cross: "In this is love...," "For God so loved...," "God demonstrated His love...," etc. (See John 3:16; Romans 5:5,6,8; Ephesians 2:4,5; 5:2,25; 1 John 3:16; 4:10; and Revelation 1:5, among others.) The cross is the focal point of God's love for the world.

Those who look to the cross as a token of God's love will never doubt His steadfast devotion to them, regardless of their circumstances. But those who come to Christ seeking a wonderful life will think that their happiness is evidence of God's love, and therefore when trials come and their happiness leaves they may think that God has forsaken them—or worse, that He doesn't exist.

For example, consider this excerpt from an article titled "Is There Happiness without Jesus?" by Merle Hertzler. This article reveals the common and bitter fruit of preaching the "happiness" gospel:

> Much of the Bible is false. God never visited this world as a man. We are on our own in this world, without direct intervention from God. So it would seem to me.
>
> How do you react to those statements? Does it make you feel sad to think that someone would write them? Perhaps to you, Christ is the only hope in this world. Your life is centered on him. He is your purpose in life. He is your Lord and your Redeemer. I understand. I have been there. I accepted Jesus Christ as my personal savior many years ago. I have read the Bible from cover to cover six times— every chapter, every verse, and every line...I have been there and done that...I know the excitement of doing God's work all day Sunday. And I also know the emptiness that would come on Monday...
>
> I am no longer a Christian. I am no longer marching in the Christian army, for I have found something different...Life without Christianity can

be far more fulfilling than anything that I had ever found inside of Christianity. And there are hundreds of others who testify to the same thing. I am not a Christian, and I am happy...

Perhaps you have indeed found genuine happiness in Christianity. I am glad for you. I hope you understand that others have found happiness elsewhere. You may not need what I have to be happy, and I may not need what you have.[39]

What a tragedy that he thought the precious blood of the Savior was shed simply to make him happy in this life, rather than to make him prepared for the next one. It does not appear this man was told about his real need— to repent or he would perish (see Luke 13:3).

If the "happy" life is different from the "abundant" life Jesus offers, who is going to listen if we are blatantly honest about the persecution promised for "*all* who desire to live godly in Christ Jesus" (2 Timothy 3:12)? Certainly not as many as are attracted by the talk of a wonderful plan. What, then, is the answer to this dilemma? How are we to bring sinners to the Savior? We will address this in the next chapter.

Chapter 4

THE LOST KEY

As a brand new convert, and an avid surfer, I told my buddies I had found something that was better than surfing. They couldn't believe there could be any such thing, but with my continual hounding, a number decided to experiment and prayed the "sinner's prayer." Not because they realized they had sinned against God and were repentant, but because they wanted to see if what I was saying was true. Within a very short time, almost all fell away from the faith, much to my dismay. I never fully understood why this happened until August 1982.

One Friday afternoon I was sitting in my office reading a portion of a sermon by Charles Spurgeon. I was fascinated to find that the "Prince of Preachers" used God's Law (the Ten Commandments) to cause his hearers to tremble. This is what I read that began a radical change in my life:

> There is a war between you and God's Law. The Ten Commandments are against you. The First comes forward and says, "Let him be cursed, for he denies Me. He has another god beside Me. His god is his belly and he yields his homage to his lust." All the Ten Commandments, like ten great cannons, are pointed at you today. For you have broken all of

God's statutes and lived in daily neglect of His Commandments.

Soul, you will find it a hard thing to go at war with the Law. When the Law came in peace, Sinai was altogether on a smoke and even Moses said, "I exceedingly fear and quake!" What will you do when the Law of God comes in terror; when the trumpet of the archangel shall tear you from your grave; when the eyes of God shall burn their way into your guilty soul; when the great books shall be opened and all your shame and sin shall be published? Can you stand against an angry Law in that day?

A few days later as I was reading Galatians 3:24, the question suddenly struck me: Is it legitimate to use the Law as a schoolmaster to bring sinners to Christ, just as it brought Israel to Christ? I closed my Bible and began to search for a sinner on whom I could experiment.

I began to understand the great principle that the Law was a schoolmaster that brings the knowledge of sin, convincing a sinner of his need for the Savior.

When I found a gentleman who was open to conversation, I took him through the Ten Commandments first, and *then* I shared the cross. He stood to his feet and said, "I've never heard anyone put that so clearly in all my life!" It was like a light went on in both of our heads. He understood the gospel, and I began to understand the great principle that the Law was a schoolmaster that brings the knowledge of sin, convincing a sinner of his need for the Savior.

I immediately began to study Scripture as well as the gospel proclamation of men like John Wesley, Spurgeon,

Whitefield, Moody, Luther, and others whom God had used down through the ages. I found they used a principle that is almost entirely neglected by modern evangelical methods. They warned that if the Law wasn't used to prepare the way for the gospel, those who made decisions for Christ would almost certainly be false in their profession and would fall away.

The Purpose of the Law

When I speak of using the Law[40] in evangelism, I don't mean merely making a casual reference to it. Rather, the Law should be the backbone of our gospel presentation, because its function is to prepare the sinner's heart for grace. Martin Luther said of the Law, "In its true and proper work and purpose it humbles a man and prepares him—if he uses the Law correctly—to yearn and seek for grace."

The Bible tells us in 1 Timothy 1:8 (AMP), "Now we recognize and know that the Law is good if anyone uses it lawfully [for the purpose for which it was designed]." For what purpose was God's Law designed? The following verse tells us: "The Law is not made for a righteous person, but...for sinners" (1 Timothy 1:9). It then even lists the sinners for us: murderers, fornicators, homosexuals, kidnappers, liars, etc. (vv. 9,10). The Law's main design is not for the saved, but for the unsaved. It was given primarily as an evangelistic tool, as a schoolmaster to bring us to Christ. D. L. Moody said, "The Law can only chase a man to Calvary, no further."

However, it is an unlawful use of the Law to try to use it for justification. No one will make it to Heaven by keeping the Ten Commandments. The Scriptures make that very clear: "A man is not justified by the works of the law but by faith in Jesus Christ . . . ; for by the works of the law no flesh shall be justified" (Galatians 2:16). Salvation is by grace alone, through faith alone, in Christ alone. The Law's rightful purpose is simply to act as a mirror to show us that we need cleansing. Those who seek to be justified by the Law are taking the mirror off the wall and trying to wash themselves with it.

Used correctly (lawfully), the Law is the rod and staff of the shepherd to guide the sheep to himself. It is the net of the fisherman, the plow of the farmer. It is the ten golden trumpets that prepare the way for the King. The Law makes the sinner thirst for righteousness, that he might live. Its holy light reveals the dust of sin on the table of the human heart, so that the gospel in the hand of the Spirit can wipe it perfectly clean.

In Numbers 21:6–9, God sent fiery serpents among the Israelites, causing them to admit that they had sinned. When the people turned to God in repentance, He instructed Moses to craft a bronze serpent and place it on a pole where the people could see it. Those who had been bitten and were doomed to die could look at the bronze serpent and live. In John 3:14, Jesus specifically cites this Old Testament passage in reference to His impending sacrifice on the cross to purchase our salvation from sin. The Ten Commandments are like ten biting serpents that carry with them the venomous curse of the Law. They drive sinners to look to the One lifted up on the cross. If the Law of Moses did not demand death for sin, Jesus would not have had to die. The Messiah became a curse for us and redeemed us from the curse of the Law (see Galatians 3:13).

The Old Testament said that the Messiah would "magnify the law and make it honorable" (Isaiah 42:21). The religious leaders had demeaned and dishonored God's Law. By their tradition, they had twisted its ordinances, rendering it ineffectual (see Matthew 15:6). They had "neglected the weightier matters of the Law," limiting the scope of its precepts to mere outward piety (see Matthew 23:23). In doing so, they had nullified the Law's power to accomplish its purpose: bringing people to the knowledge of their sinfulness and their need for repentance and salvation.

They even hindered others from entering God's kingdom. This is what Jesus said to them: "Woe to you lawyers! For you have taken away the key of knowledge. You did not enter in yourselves, and those who were entering in you hindered" (Luke 11:52). These lawyers were professing to be experts in God's Law. But because they did not use the "key of knowledge" to bring sinners to the Savior, they hindered the work of the Law as a "groundbreaking" instrument in people's hearts.

So Jesus first straightened out what the religious leaders had bent, and honored what they had demeaned:

> "Do not think that I came to destroy the Law or the Prophets. I did not come to destroy but to fulfill. For assuredly, I say to you, till heaven and earth pass away, one jot or one tittle will by no means pass from the law till all is fulfilled. Whoever therefore breaks one of the least of these commandments, and teaches men so, shall be called least in the kingdom of heaven; but whoever does and teaches them, he shall be called great in the kingdom of heaven. For I say to you, that unless your righteousness exceeds the righteousness of the scribes and Pharisees,

you will by no means enter the kingdom of heaven."
(Matthew 5:17–20)

Next, Jesus opened up the spiritual nature of the Law,
showing how God "desire[s] truth in the inward parts"
(Psalm 51:6). God will judge not only the actions but the
thoughts and intents of the heart. Notice how Jesus magnifies the Sixth and the Seventh Commandments:

> "You have heard that it was said to those of old, 'You
> shall not murder, and whoever murders will be in
> danger of the judgment.' But I say to you that who-
> ever is angry with his brother without a cause shall
> be in danger of the judgment. And whoever says to
> his brother, 'Raca!' shall be in danger of the council.
> But whoever says, 'You fool!' shall be in danger of
> hell fire... You have heard that it was said to those
> of old, 'You shall not commit adultery.' But I say to
> you that whoever looks at a woman to lust for her has
> already committed adultery with her in his heart."
> (Matthew 5:21,22,27,28)

Later in this same discourse, Jesus magnified the Law
further by opening up the Ninth Commandment:

> "Again you have heard that it was said to those of
> old, 'You shall not swear falsely, but shall perform
> your oaths to the Lord.' But I say to you, do not swear
> at all: neither by heaven, for it is God's throne; nor by
> the earth, for it is His footstool; nor by Jerusalem,
> for it is the city of the great King. Nor shall you
> swear by your head, because you cannot make one
> hair white or black. But let your 'Yes' be 'Yes,' and
> your 'No,' 'No.' For whatever is more than these is
> from the evil one." (Matthew 5:33–37)

Jesus concluded by saying, "Be perfect, just as your Father in heaven is perfect" (Matthew 5:48). This statement must have left His hearers speechless—which is likely what Jesus intended, because the function of the Law is "that every mouth may be stopped, and all the world may become guilty before God" (Romans 3:19).

Who can justify themselves in God's sight if we are commanded to be perfect? No one. Our mouths are stopped and we see our guilt. Some Bible commentators have suggested that Jesus didn't really mean "perfect," as in "without defect, flawless." Instead, they contend that He was telling us to be mature. However, then Jesus would be saying, "You are to be mature, as your heavenly Father is mature." Calling God "mature" would imply that He was once immature. But God never changes (Malachi 3:6). He has always been perfect and doesn't need to mature. His Law is also perfect, and if we are not perfect in accordance with the Law, we will perish on the Day of Judgment. That's why Paul says we are to "[warn] every man and [teach] every man in all wisdom, that we may present every man perfect in Christ Jesus" (Colossians 1:28).

Scripture makes clear that it is the perfect Law of God that actually converts the soul: "The law of the Lord is perfect, converting the soul" (Psalm 19:7). Matthew Henry says, "Of this excellent use is the Law: it converts the soul, opens the eyes, prepares the way of the Lord in the desert, rends the rocks, levels the mountains, makes a people prepared for the Lord."

The Offense and the Foolishness of the Cross

According to Scripture, "[the real function of] the Law is to make men recognize and be conscious of sin [not mere perception, but an acquaintance with sin which works toward repentance...]" (Romans 3:20, AMP). To illustrate this point, let's look for a moment at civil law. Imagine if I said to you, "I have some good news for you. Someone has just paid a $25,000 speeding fine on your behalf!" You would probably respond with some cynicism in your voice, "What are you talking about? That's not good news; it doesn't make sense. I don't *have* a $25,000 speeding fine." Your reaction would be quite understandable. If you do not know that you have broken the law in the first place, the good news of someone paying a fine for you will not be good news; it will be foolishness to you. But more than that, it would be offensive to you, because I am insinuating that you have broken the law when you don't think you have.

However, if I were to put it this way it may make more sense: "Today, a law enforcement officer clocked you traveling at fifty-five miles an hour in an area designated for a blind children's convention. There were ten clear warning signs indicating that the maximum speed was fifteen miles an hour, but you completely ignored them and went straight through at fifty-five miles an hour. What you did was extremely dangerous. The penalty is a $25,000 fine or imprisonment."

As you begin to see the seriousness of what you have done, I explain, "The law was about to take its course when someone you don't even know stepped in and paid the fine for you. You are very fortunate."

Can you see that telling you precisely what you have done wrong *first* actually makes the good news make sense? If I don't clearly bring instruction and understanding that you have violated the law, then the good news will seem foolishness; it will seem offensive. But once you understand that you have broken the law, then the good news that your penalty has been paid will become good news indeed.

In the same way, if I approach an impenitent sinner and say, "Jesus Christ died on the cross for your sins," it will be foolishness and offensive to him. It will be foolishness because it won't make sense. The Bible tells us that: "The preaching of the cross is foolishness to those who are perishing" (1 Corinthians 1:18). And it will be offensive because I am insinuating that he is a sinner when he doesn't think he is. As far as he is concerned, there are a lot of people far worse than him.

> *Once you understand that you have broken the law, then the good news that your penalty has been paid will become good news indeed.*

But if I take the time to follow in the footsteps of Jesus, it may make more sense. If I open up the divine Law, the Ten Commandments, to show the sinner precisely what he has done wrong—that he has offended God by violating His Law—then he will become "convicted by the law as a transgressor" (James 2:9). Once he understands his transgression, the good news of his penalty being paid will not be foolishness, nor will it be offensive. It will be "the power of God to salvation" (Romans 1:16).

With that in mind, let's look at some of the functions of God's Law for humanity. Romans 3:19 says, "Now we know that whatever the law says, it says to those who are under the law, that every mouth may be stopped, and all the world may become guilty before God." So one function of God's Law is to stop the mouth, to stop sinners from justifying themselves and saying, "There are plenty of people worse than me. I'm not a bad person, really." The Law stops the mouth of justification and leaves not just the Jews, but the whole world guilty before God.

Romans 3:20 says, "Therefore by the deeds of the law no flesh will be justified in His sight, for *by the law is the knowledge of sin*." It is God's Law that tells us what sin is. So if you want sinners to see their need for forgiveness, use the Law to show them their sin. In fact, 1 John 3:4 gives us the biblical definition of sin: "sin is lawlessness," or as the King James translation puts it, "sin is the transgression of the law." In Romans 7:7, Paul asks, "What shall we say then? Is the law sin? Certainly not! On the contrary, *I would not have known sin except through the law*. For I would not have known covetousness unless the law had said, 'You shall not covet.'" Paul is reiterating, "I didn't know what sin was *until the Law told me*." Since the definition of sin is the transgression of the Law, according to Scripture, the only way people can know their sin is by seeing themselves in light of the Moral Law.

The wonderful thing about God's Law is that God has written it upon our heart. Romans 2:15 says, "who show the work of the law written in their hearts, their conscience also bearing witness, and between themselves their thoughts accusing or else excusing them." The word *conscience* means "with knowledge." *Con* is "with," *science* is "knowledge." So each time we lie, steal, blaspheme, commit adultery, etc., we do it *with knowledge* that it is wrong. God has given light to every man. Society may *shape* our conscience, but God is its Giver, and no society (regardless of how primitive) has been left in complete moral darkness. This is why the Law is so effective universally. The conscience *echoes* the Commandments. It bears witness.

For this reason, according to Martin Luther, "The first duty of the gospel preacher is to declare God's Law and show the nature of sin." Martyn Lloyd-Jones said, "The trouble with people who are not seeking for a Savior, and for salvation, is that they do not understand the nature of sin. It is the peculiar function of the Law to bring such an understanding to a man's mind and conscience. That is why great evangelical preachers 300 years ago in the time of the Puritans, and 200 years ago in the time of Whitefield and others, always engaged in what they called a preliminary law work."

When we use the Law to appeal to the conscience and bring the knowledge of sin, we merely work with the Holy Spirit to convince people of their transgression. Jesus said that the Holy Spirit "will convict the world of sin, and of righteousness, and of judgment" (John 16:8). Scripture tells us that *sin* is transgression of the Law (1 John 3:4), *righteousness* is of the Law (Romans 10:5), and *judgment* is by the Law (Romans 2:12; James 2:12).

Since He alone brings conviction, and He has chosen to do this through "the foolishness of preaching" (1 Corinthians 1:21), we must have absolute reliance on the Holy Spirit for the conversion of the lost. Without the Holy Spirit, anything we preach is nothing but dead letter. Billy Graham said, "The Holy Spirit convicts us... He shows us the Ten Commandments; the Law is the schoolmaster that leads us to Christ." Spurgeon adds, "When the Holy Spirit comes to us, He shows us what the Law really is." Paris Reidhead warned, "When 100 years ago earnest scholars decreed that the Law had no relationship to the preaching of the gospel, they deprived the Holy Spirit in the area where their influence prevailed of the only instrument with which He had ever armed Himself to prepare sinners for grace."

If the Law has no part in bringing a sinner to Christ, why did Paul so often say that the Law was instrumental in his conversion? He didn't say, "I would not have known sin except *through the Holy Spirit*," or "*By the Holy Spirit* is the knowledge of sin," or that *through the Holy Spirit* sin became "exceedingly sinful." Instead he said that it was *the Law* (in the hand of the Spirit) that produced this state of conviction (see Romans 3:20; 7:7; 7:13).

John Wesley observed:

> It is the ordinary method of the Spirit of God to convict sinners by the law. It is this, which, being set home on the conscience, generally breaketh the rocks in pieces. It is more especially this part of the Word of God which is quick and powerful, full of life and energy, "and sharper than any two-edged sword."... By this is the sinner discovered to himself. All his fig leaves are torn away, and he sees that he is "wretched, and poor, and miserable, and blind, and naked." The law flashes conviction on every side. He feels himself a mere sinner. He has nothing to pay. His "mouth is stopped," and he stands "guilty before God."

The use of the Law in evangelism is the neglected key to the sinner's heart, in order for there to be conviction and conversion. Many of us in the past have wanted to avoid making sinners feel guilty. Yet the reality is that they *are* "guilty before God." In the next chapter we are going to look at why bringing the knowledge of sin is an essential step in preparing the heart for grace.

Chapter 5

Making Grace Amazing

From the moment of my conversion, I have been vainly trying to find words to describe the insanity of a dying world rejecting God's gift of everlasting life. In a sense, man has a God-shaped hole in his head. It's only when the Holy Spirit rushes in that we receive a sound mind (see 2 Timothy 1:7). We insanely run at Hell as though it were Heaven, and reject Heaven as though it were Hell itself. I am eternally thankful to God for His amazing grace, which reached down one dark night in 1972 and saved a wretch like me. We long for others to have that same thankfulness, but unbelievers cannot comprehend God's grace until they recognize their guilt. As John MacArthur noted:

> God's grace cannot be faithfully preached to unbelievers until the Law is preached and man's corrupt nature is exposed. It is impossible for a person to fully realize his need for God's grace until he sees how terribly he has failed the standards of God's Law.

In Romans 5:20, Paul explains further why God's Law entered the scene: "Moreover the law entered that the offense might abound. But where sin abounded, grace abounded much more." When sin abounds, grace abounds *much more*; and according to Scripture, the thing that makes sin abound is the Law.

Again, we can see the work of God's Law illustrated in civil law. Watch what often happens on a freeway when there is no visible sign of law enforcement. See how motorists exceed the speed limit. It would seem that each speeder thinks to himself that the law has forgotten to patrol his part of the freeway. He is transgressing the law by only fifteen miles an hour—and besides, he isn't the only one doing it.

Notice, however, what happens when the law enters the fast lane with red lights flashing. The speeder's heart misses a beat. He is no longer secure in the fact that other motorists are also speeding. He knows that he is *personally* guilty, and he could be the one the officer pulls over. Suddenly, his "mere" fifteen-mile-per-hour transgression doesn't seem such a small thing after all. It seems to abound.

Look at the freeway of sin. The whole world naturally goes with the flow. Who hasn't had a lustful thought at one time or another? Who in today's society doesn't tell the occasional "white" lie? Who hasn't taken something that belongs to someone else, even if it's just a "white-collar" crime? They know they are doing wrong, but their security lies in the fact that so many others are just as guilty, if not more so. It seems that God has forgotten all about sin and the Ten Commandments. The sinner "has said in his heart, 'God has forgotten; He hides His face; He will never see'" (Psalm 10:11).

Now watch the Law enter with red lights flashing. The sinner's heart skips a beat. He examines the speedometer of his conscience. Suddenly, it shows him the measure of his guilt in a new light—the light of the Law. His sense of security in the fact that there are multitudes doing the same thing becomes irrelevant, because every man will give an account of himself to God (see Romans 14:12). Sin not only becomes personal, it seems to "abound." The Law shows him that his mere lust becomes adultery of the heart (see Matthew 5:27,28); his white lie becomes false witness; his own way becomes rebellion and a violation of the First Commandment; his hatred becomes murder in God's sight (see 1 John 3:15); his "sticky" fingers make him a thief. "Moreover the law entered that the offense might abound." Without the entrance of the Law, sin is neither personal, nor is it a threat: "For without the Law sin is dead [the sense of it is inactive and a lifeless thing]" (Romans 7:8, AMP).

It is the Commandment that shows sin in its true light, that it is "exceedingly sinful" (Romans 7:13). The guilty sinner places his hand on his mouth, with nothing to say in his defense. As he understands the seriousness of his sins in God's eyes, he now sees his need for the Savior. In Galatians 3:24 we read that "the law was our schoolmaster to bring us to Christ, that we might be justified by faith" (KJV). God's Law serves as a schoolmaster, or tutor, to bring us to Jesus Christ so we can be justified through faith in His blood.

As John R. Stott said, "We cannot come to Christ to be justified until we have first been to Moses, to be condemned. But once we have gone to Moses, and acknowledged our sin, guilt and condemnation, we must not stay there. We must let Moses send us to Christ." The Law doesn't help us; it just leaves us helpless. It doesn't justify us; it just leaves us guilty before the judgment bar of a holy God.

The tragedy is that just over one hundred years ago, when the Church forsook the Law in its capacity to bring the knowledge of sin and drive sinners to Christ, it therefore had to find another reason for sinners to respond to the gospel. Modern evangelism chose to attract sinners using the issue of "life enhancement." The gospel degenerated into "Jesus Christ will give you peace, joy, love, fulfillment, and lasting happiness." To Martyn Lloyd-Jones, one of the most influential preachers of the twentieth century, this is not evangelism at all:

> There is no true evangelism without the doctrine of sin, and without an understanding of what sin is. I do not want to be unfair, but I say that a gospel which merely says, "Come to Jesus," and offers Him as a Friend, and offers a marvelous new life, without convicting of sin, is not New Testament evangelism. The essence of evangelism is to start by preaching the Law; and it is because the Law has not been preached that we have had so much superficial evangelism. True evangelism . . . must always start by preaching the Law.

Sadly, we have moved away from "true evangelism" by preaching a gospel of grace without first convincing men that they are transgressors. Consequently, many people I witness to claim to have been born-again three or four times, so that statements like this are commonplace: "I got saved when I was six, then again at twelve. I then fell away, got into some bad stuff, and came back to the Lord when I was twenty-three." It's very apparent that the person is not a Christian. He admits to being a fornicator, liar, and blasphemer, and has no desire for the things of God, but he thinks he is saved because he has been "born again." He is using the grace of our God for an occasion of the flesh. For him it's not a bad thing to trample the blood of Christ underfoot (see Hebrews 10:29). Why? Because he has never been convinced of the disease of sin that he might appreciate the cure of the gospel.

According to Paris Reidhead, "We have gospel-hardened a generation of sinners by telling them how to be saved before they have any understanding why they need to be saved." Reidhead simply believed that we should not prescribe the cure before we have convinced of the disease. He was not alone in this thought. D. L. Moody states:

> *"A gospel which merely says, 'Come to Jesus,' and offers a marvelous new life, without convicting of sin, is not New Testament evangelism."*

It is a great mistake to give a man who has not been convicted of sin certain passages that were never meant for him. The Law is what he needs... Do not offer the consolation of the gospel until he sees and knows he is guilty before God. We must give enough of the Law to take away all self-righteousness. I pity the man who preaches only one side of the truth— always the gospel, and never the Law.

When we set aside the Law of God and its designed function to convert the soul, we remove the very means by which sinners are able to see their need for God's forgiveness. Matthew Henry stated, "As that which is straight discovers that which is crooked, as the looking-glass shows us our natural face with all its spots and deformities, so there is no way of coming to that knowledge of sin which is necessary to repentance, and consequently to peace and pardon, but by comparing our hearts and lives with the Law." John Bunyan, author of *Pilgrim's Progress*, noted, "The man who does not know the nature of the Law, cannot know the nature of sin."

What "Sin" Are You Talking About?

When David sinned with Bathsheba, he broke every one of the Ten Commandments. He coveted his neighbor's wife, lived a lie, stole her, committed adultery, murdered her husband, dishonored his parents, and thus broke the remaining four Commandments in reference to his relationship with God. So, the Lord sent Nathan the prophet to reprove him (see 2 Samuel 12:1–13).

There is great significance in the order in which the reproof came. Nathan gave David, the shepherd of Israel, a parable about something that he could understand—sheep. Nathan began with the natural realm rather than immediately exposing the king's sin. He told a story about a rich man who, instead of taking a sheep from his own flock, killed a poor man's pet lamb to feed a stranger.

David was indignant and sat up on his high throne of self-righteousness. He revealed his knowledge of the Law by saying that the guilty party should restore fourfold for the lamb and should die for his crime. Nathan then exposed the king's sin of taking another man's "lamb," saying, "You are the man! . . . Why have you despised the commandment of the LORD, to do evil in His sight?" When David cried, "I have sinned against the LORD," the prophet then gave him grace and said, "The LORD also has put away your sin; you shall not die."

Imagine if Nathan, fearful of rejection, decided to change things around a little and added a few of his own thoughts. He instead says to the king, "God loves you and has a wonderful plan for your life. However, there is something that is keeping you from enjoying this wonderful plan; it is called sin."

Imagine if he had glossed over the personal nature of David's sin with a general reference to all men having sinned and fallen short of the glory of God. David's reaction might have been, "What 'sin' are you talking about?" rather than to admit his terrible transgression. Think of it. Why should he say, "I have sinned against the LORD" after hearing that message? Instead, in a sincere desire to experience this "wonderful plan," he might have admitted that he, like all men, had sinned and fallen short of God's glory.

If David had not been made to tremble under the wrath of the Law, the prophet would have removed the very means of producing godly sorrow, which was so necessary for David's repentance. It is conviction of sin that causes godly sorrow, and "godly sorrow produces repentance to salvation" (2 Corinthians 7:10). It was the weight of David's *personal* guilt that caused him to cry out, "I have sinned against the LORD." The Law caused him to labor and become heavy laden; it made him hunger and thirst for righteousness. It enlightened him about the serious nature of sin as far as God was concerned.

In *Today's Gospel: Authentic or Synthetic?* Walter Chantry writes:

> The absence of God's holy Law from modern preaching is perhaps as responsible as any other factor for the evangelistic impotence of our churches and missions. Only by the light of the Law can the vermin of sin in the heart be exposed. Satan has effectively used a very clever device to silence the

Law, which is needed as an instrument to bring perishing men to Christ.

It is imperative that preachers of today learn how to declare the spiritual Law of God; for, until we learn how to wound consciences, we shall have no wounds to bind with gospel bandages.

George Whitefield, possibly the most famous religious figure of the eighteenth century, understood the necessity of presenting the Law before the gospel: "First, then, before you can speak peace to your hearts, you must be made to see, made to feel, made to weep over, made to bewail, your actual transgressions against the Law of God."

Unspeakable Gratitude

When Nathan then brought the good news that David would not die, that God had put away his sin, do you think the guilty king was relieved? Do you think he was grateful to God for His mercy? I think that he would have been unspeakably grateful. What do you think made him appreciate that mercy? Wouldn't it have been the fact that he, in the light of Nathan's rebuke, suddenly saw the reality of his guilt? The more David understood his personal guilt before God, the more he appreciated free mercy. If he had been left thinking lightly of his sin, he would have thought lightly of God's mercy.

This is why it is essential to expound the Law with a sinner, and to make him feel his personal guilt. The sinner has sinned against God by violating His Law a multitude of times, and he is an enemy of God in his mind through wicked works (see Colossians 1:21). The reality is that "God is angry with the wicked every day" (Psalm 7:11) and that God's wrath abides on them (see John 3:36).

With each transgression, sinners are "treasuring up for [themselves] wrath in the day of wrath" (Romans 2:5).

Perhaps you are tempted to say that we should never condemn sinners by using the Law. However, Scripture tells us that they are *already* condemned: "He who does not believe is condemned already" (John 3:18). All the Law does is show them their true state. If you dust a table in your living room and think it is dust-free, try pulling back the curtains and letting in the early morning sunlight. You will more than likely see dust still sitting on the table. The sunlight didn't create the dust; it merely exposed it. When we take the time to draw back the high and heavy curtains of the Holy of Holies and let the light of God's Law shine upon the sinner's heart, the Law merely shows him his true state before God. Proverbs 6:23 tells us, "The commandment is a lamp, and the law a light."

As the sinner sits as king on the throne of self-righteousness, deceived by sin, you are to be a Nathan to him and say, "You are the man." The more understanding he has of his sin, the more he will appreciate the mercy of the cross. "If men do not understand the Law," explained Charles Spurgeon, "they will not feel that they are sinners. And if they are not consciously sinners, they will never value the sin offering. There is no healing a man till the Law has wounded him, no making him alive till the Law has slain him."

After Kirk Cameron first heard this teaching on the use of the Law he sent me the following email:

> Ray,
> I was so fired up after leaving your place! Your teachings on the Law and grace have made more sense to me than anyone else's, and I am so thankful for

what God is doing...I believe I was robbed of the deep pain of seeing the depth of my sinfulness, of experiencing the exceeding joy and gratitude that comes from the cross, because I was convinced of God's love before I was convinced of my sin. I didn't see the big problem, but by faith believed I was a sinner (many worse than me, but nevertheless a sinner), and repented of my "general sinful, selfish attitude." I had never opened up the Ten Commandments and looked deep into the well of my sinful heart. I never imagined that God was actually angry with me at a certain point because of my sin. Because of "grace," I kind of skipped over that part and was just thankful that He loved me and had promised me eternal life.

The Law-less message that "God has a wonderful plan for your life" doesn't cause sinners to tremble and cry out, "I have sinned against God!"

While I think I was saved thirteen years ago, I was rocked out of my chair last night, on my knees confessing the specific sins that have plagued my heart that were never uncovered before. I think my knowledge of the "new covenant" and "under grace, not Law" kept me from ever examining my heart by the light of the Ten Commandments. The new weight of my sin is causing more pain in me...wounding my ego, and showing me how much more Jesus had to pay to set me free. Oh, the wonderful cross!!!!

The Law-less message that "God has a wonderful plan for your life" does not cause sinners to tremble and cry out, "I have sinned against God!" Though they may acknowledge that, like all men, they fall short of the glory of God, it does not show them the serious nature of their personal transgression. Consequently, the depth of their sorrow is in proportion to their shallow understanding of the seriousness of their sin. They do not experience a godly sorrow that is necessary for repentance. However, when we help sinners see the depth of their sin in light of a perfect Law, it makes God's grace truly amazing.

Paradoxical as it may seem, the Law makes grace abound, in the same way that darkness makes light shine. It was John Newton, the writer of "Amazing Grace," who said, "Ignorance of the nature and design of the Law is at the bottom of most religious mistakes," warning that a wrong understanding of the harmony between Law and grace would produce "error on the left and the right hand." I don't know whether any of us could claim to have a better understanding of grace than the one who penned such a hymn.

What I am saying is not some new doctrine. The use of the Law in evangelism is rooted both in Scripture and in Church history. The enemy has hidden it, and that has created havoc within Christendom. In *Striking Incidents of Saving Grace*, Henry Breeden tells of a preacher in Colliery, England, who saw a number of conversions take place under his ministry. Then in 1861 a "stranger" passed through and conducted meetings in which "there were great numbers of persons" who professed faith in Jesus. The preacher then recounts the sad effects:

> But many of them were, in a short time, gone back again into the world. Indeed, so complete was the failure that the Minister who succeeded me in that Circuit said, "There was not one single person, out

of about ninety who professed to obtain Religion through that man's services, that continued to be a member of the Colliery Church."

I had observed the same sort of thing before in regard to the efforts of suchlike persons in other places. And, therefore, I was very desirous to find out what was the cause of such failures. I was sure that the persons, said to be brought in under my own ministry, had nearly all of them held on their way, and were then members—either in the Church above, or in the Church below. So I set myself calmly to consider the whole affair. In doing this, I soon found that the preaching that does not address the sinner's conscience, and strive to break the unconverted spirit down by enforcing the Law of God, scarcely ever leads to the salvation of the soul. And these men scarcely ever preach the Law.

Yes, that is it, and nothing else—"By the Law is the knowledge of sin." Let a minister get that important sentiment burnt into his very soul by the Light and flaming Love of God. And then let him go forth and preach the truth as it is in Jesus, and many, many precious souls will soon be saved. But let him omit preaching the Law, and whatever else he may do— for he can accomplish many great things—yet, under that man's ministry, conversions will be scarce.[41]

I couldn't give a heartier "Amen!" to his conclusion: "Yes, that is it, and nothing else—'By the Law is the knowledge of sin.'" This teaching is so foundational, and yet we have failed to see its simple truth. In the next chapter we are going to look at the importance of a sinner's motive in responding to the gospel.

Chapter 6

THE MOTIVE AND THE RESULT

S o far we have looked at the dismal moral state of contemporary Christianity. We have seen that there are millions within the Church who do not have the "things that accompany salvation" (Hebrews 6:9), and multitudes of others who have fallen away from the faith. This has happened because the Law has not been used to bring the knowledge of sin. Instead, we have used an unbiblical method of attracting sinners to a "wonderful new life in Christ." We are now going to look closely at what happens to the sinner's motive when this modern method is used. Consider the following scenario.

Two men are seated in a plane. The first is given a parachute and told to put it on because it will improve his flight. He is a little skeptical at first; he cannot see how wearing a parachute on board a plane could possibly improve his flight.

After some time, he decides to experiment and see if the claims are true. As he straps the apparatus to his back, he notices the weight of it on his shoulders and he finds he now has difficulty sitting upright. However, he consoles himself with the flight attendant's promise that the parachute will improve his flight, and he decides to give it a little time.

As the flight progresses, he notices that some of the other passengers are laughing at him because he is wearing a parachute inside the plane. He begins to feel somewhat humiliated. As they continue to laugh and point at him, he can stand it no longer. He sinks in his seat, unstraps the parachute, and throws it to the floor. Disillusionment and bitterness fill his heart because as far as he is concerned, he was told an outright lie.

The second man is also given a parachute, *but listen to what he is told*. He is told to put it on because at any moment he will have to jump out of the plane at 25,000 feet. He gratefully puts the parachute on. He does not notice the weight of it upon his shoulders, nor is he concerned that he cannot sit upright. His mind is consumed with the thought of what would happen to him if he jumped without the parachute.

Let's now analyze the motive and the result of each passenger's experience. The first man's motive for putting on the parachute was solely to improve his flight. The result of his experience was that he was humiliated by the other passengers, disillusioned, and somewhat embittered against those who gave him the parachute. As far as he is concerned, it will be a long time before anyone gets one of those things on his back again.

The second man put on the parachute solely to survive the jump to come. And because of his knowledge of what would happen to him if he jumped without it, he has a deep-rooted joy and peace in his heart, knowing that he has been saved from certain death. This knowledge gives him the ability to withstand the mockery of the other passengers. His attitude toward those who gave him the parachute is one of heartfelt gratitude.

Many modern evangelistic appeals say, "Put on the Lord Jesus Christ. He'll give you love, joy, peace, fulfillment, and lasting happiness." In other words, Jesus will improve your flight. The sinner responds, and in an experimental fashion puts on the Savior to see if the claims are true. And what does he get? The promised temptation, tribulation, and persecution. He finds it difficult to live an upright life. Not only that, but other people mock him for his faith. So what does he do? He takes off the Lord Jesus Christ; he is offended for the Word's sake; he is disillusioned and somewhat embittered—and quite rightly so. He was promised love, joy, peace, fulfillment, and lasting happiness, and all he got were trials and humiliation. His bitterness is directed toward those who gave him the so-called Good News. Because he thinks he tried Jesus and it didn't work out, his latter end becomes worse than the first—he is now another inoculated and bitter "backslider."

Instead of preaching that Jesus will "improve the flight," we should be warning sinners that one day they will have to jump out of the plane.

Instead of preaching that Jesus will "improve the flight," we should be warning sinners that one day they will have to jump out of the plane. "It is appointed for men to die once, but after this the judgment" (Hebrews 9:27). When a sinner understands the horrific consequences of breaking the Law of God, he will flee to the Savior in genuine repentance, solely to escape the wrath that is to come. If we are true and faithful witnesses, that is what we will be preaching—that there is wrath to come, and that God "commands all men everywhere to repent, *because* He has appointed a day on which He will judge the world in righteousness" (Acts 17:30,31). The issue is not one of *happiness* but one of *righteousness*.

It does not matter how happy a sinner is or how much he is enjoying the pleasures of sin for a season; without the righteousness of Christ, he will perish on the day of wrath. The Bible says, "Riches do not profit in the day of wrath, but righteousness delivers from death" (Proverbs 11:4). Peace and joy are legitimate *fruits* of salvation, but it is not legitimate to use these fruits as a drawing card *for* salvation. If we do, the sinner will respond with an impure motive, lacking repentance.

Can you remember why the second passenger had joy and peace in his heart? It was because he knew that the parachute was going to save him from certain death. In the same way, as Christians we have "joy and peace in believing" (Romans 15:13) because we know that the righteousness of Christ is going to deliver us from the wrath to come.

With that thought in mind, let's take a look at another incident aboard the plane. We have a brand new flight attendant. It is her first day, and she is carrying a tray of boiling hot coffee. As she is walking down the aisle, she trips over someone's foot and slops the hot coffee all over the lap of our second passenger. What is his reaction as that boiling liquid hits his tender flesh? Does he say, "Man, that hurt!"? Yes, he does. But does he then rip the parachute from his shoulders, throw it to the floor, and say, "That stupid parachute!"? No; why should he? He didn't put the parachute on to have a better flight. He put it on to save himself when the time comes to jump. If anything, the hot coffee incident causes him to cling tighter to the parachute and even look forward to the jump.

If we have put on the Lord Jesus Christ for the right motive—to flee from the wrath to come—when tribulation strikes, when the flight gets bumpy, when we get burned by circumstances, we won't get angry at God, and we won't lose our joy and peace. Why should we? We did not come to Christ for a better lifestyle but to flee from the wrath to come.

If anything, tribulation drives the true believer closer to the Savior. Sadly, multitudes of professing Christians lose their joy and peace when the flight gets bumpy. Why? They are products of a man-centered gospel. They came lacking repentance, without which they cannot be saved.

As Peter preached, he commanded his hearers to repent "for the remission of sins" (Acts 2:38). Without repentance, there is no remission of sins. Peter further said, "Repent therefore and be converted, that your sins may be blotted out" (Acts 3:19). We cannot be "converted" unless we repent. That is why Jesus commanded that *repentance* be preached to all nations (Luke 24:47).

Superficial Repentance

For many years I suffered from the disease of "evangelical frustration." I so wanted sinners to respond to the gospel that I unwittingly preached a man-centered message, the essence of which was this: "You'll never find true peace without Jesus Christ; you have a God-shaped hole in your heart that only He can fill." I'd preach Christ crucified; I'd preach repentance. A sinner would respond to the altar, and I'd think, *This guy wants to give his heart to Jesus and there's an excellent chance he's going to backslide. So I'd better make sure he really means it. He'd better be sincere!* So I would tell him, "Now, repeat this prayer sincerely after me and really mean it from your heart sincerely and make sure you mean it. 'Oh, God, I'm a sinner.'"

He would smack his chewing gum and say, "Uh...oh, God, I'm a sinner."

I would wonder, *Why isn't there a visible sign of contrition? There is no outward evidence that the guy is inwardly sorry for his sins.*

However, if I had known his motive, I would have seen that he was *100 percent sincere.* He really did mean his decision with all of his heart. He sincerely wanted to give this Jesus thing a go to see if he could get a buzz out of it. He had tried sex, drugs, materialism, alcohol. Why not give Christianity a try and see if it's as good as all these Christians say it is: peace, joy, love, fulfillment, lasting happiness?

He wasn't fleeing from the wrath to come, because *I hadn't told him there was wrath to come.* There was a glaring omission from my message. He was not broken in contrition, because the poor guy did not know what sin was. Remember Romans 7:7? Paul said, "I would not have known sin *except through the law.*" How can a man repent of his sin if he doesn't know what sin is? Any so-called repentance would be merely what I call "horizontal repentance." A sinner may feel sorry because he has lied to men, stolen from men, etc. But when David sinned with Bathsheba, he didn't say, "I've sinned against man." He acknowledged to God, "Against You, You only, have I sinned, and done this evil in Your sight" (Psalm 51:4). When Joseph was tempted sexually, he said, "How then can I do this great wickedness, and sin against God?" (Genesis 39:9). The prodigal son admitted, "I have sinned against heaven" (Luke 15:21).

Because all sin is against God, Paul preached that we must therefore exercise "repentance toward God" (Acts 20:21)—the one whom we have offended. However, when a man doesn't understand that his sin is primarily vertical—that he has sinned against God—he will not seek His forgiveness. He will merely respond with superficial, experimental, horizontal repentance, and will fall away when tribulation, temptation, and persecution come.

The Tragic Results

If we continue to offer the Savior merely as a means of life enhancement, many will respond to the gospel for the wrong motive. To see the effect of neglecting to use the Law to bring sinners to genuine repentance, let's take a closer look at the tragic results of unbiblical methods of contemporary evangelism. These statistics represent the eternal salvation of human beings. Please read them with the same sobriety you would have while walking through a holocaust museum:

- At a 1990 crusade in the United States, 600 "decisions for Christ" were obtained. No doubt, there was much rejoicing. However, ninety days later, follow-up workers could not find even one who was continuing in the faith. That crusade created 600 "backsliders"—or, to be more scriptural, false converts.

- In Cleveland, Ohio, an inner-city outreach brought 400 decisions. The rejoicing no doubt tapered off when follow-up workers could not find a single one of the 400 who had supposedly made a decision.

- In 1991, organizers of a Salt Lake City concert encouraged follow-up and discovered, "Less than 5 percent of those who respond to an altar call during a public crusade...are living a Christian life one year later." In other words, more than 95 percent proved to be false converts.

- In 1985, a four-day crusade obtained 217 decisions. However, according to a member of the organizing committee, 92 percent fell away.

- In his book *Today's Evangelism*, Ernest C. Reisinger said of one outreach event, "It lasted eight days, and there were sixty-eight supposed conversions." A month later, not one of the "converts" could be found.

- A church in Boulder, Colorado, sent a team to Russia in 1991 and obtained 2,500 decisions. The next year, the team found only thirty continuing in their faith. That is a retention rate of 1.2 percent.

- According to Pastor Elmer Murdoch, "Chuck Colson ...states that for every 100 people making decisions for Christ, only two may return for follow-up a few days later. George Barna says that the majority of people (51 percent minimum) making decisions leave the church in 6–8 weeks."[42]

- Between 1995 and 2005, Assemblies of God churches reported an amazing 5,339,144 decisions for Christ. Their net gain in attendance was 221,790. That means that 5,117,354 (*over five million*) decisions could not be accounted for.[43]

- Charles E. Hackett, the national director of home missions for the Assemblies of God in the United States, said, "A soul at the altar does not generate much excitement in some circles because we realize approximately ninety-five out of every hundred will not become integrated into the church. In fact, most of them will not return for a second visit."

- In Sacramento, California, a combined crusade yielded more than 2,000 commitments. One church followed up on fifty-two of those decisions and could not find one true convert.

- In Leeds, England, a visiting American speaker acquired 400 decisions for a local church. Six weeks later, only two were still committed and they eventually fell away.

- In November 1970, a number of churches combined for a convention in Fort Worth, Texas, and secured 30,000 decisions. Six months later, the follow-up committee could find only thirty still continuing in their faith.

- A mass crusade reported 18,000 decisions—yet, according to *Church Growth* magazine, 94 percent failed to become incorporated into a local church.

- Pastor Dennis Grenell from Auckland, New Zealand, who has traveled to India every year since 1980, reported that he saw 80,000 decision cards stacked in a hut in the city of Rajamundry, the "results" of past evangelistic crusades. But he maintained that one would be fortunate to find even eighty Christians in the entire city.

- A leading U.S. denomination reported that during 1995 they secured 384,057 decisions but retained only 22,983 in fellowship. They could not account for 361,074 supposed conversions. That is a 94 percent fall-away rate.

- In Omaha, Nebraska, a pastor of a large church said he was involved with a crusade where 1,300 decisions were made, yet not even one "convert" was continuing in the faith.

Statistics such as these are very hard to find. What organizing committee is going to shout from the housetops that after a massive amount of pre-crusade prayer, hundreds of thousands of dollars of expenditure, preaching by a big-name evangelist, and truckloads of follow-up, the wonderful results that initially seemed apparent have all but disappeared? Not only would such news be utterly disheartening for all who put so much time and effort into the crusade, but the committee has no reasonable explanation for why the massive catch has disappeared. The statistics are therefore hushed up and swept under the carpet of "discretion."

A southern California newspaper, however, bravely printed the following article in July 1993:

> "Crusades don't do as much for nonbelievers as some might think," said Peter Wagner, professor of church growth at Fuller Theological Seminary in Pasadena. Three percent to 16 percent of those who make decisions at crusades end up responsible members of a church, he said.

In October 2002, the pastor of a large church in Colorado Springs had a similar finding:

> Only three to six percent of those who respond in a crusade end up in a local church—that's a problem...I was recently in a city that had a large crusade eighteen months earlier, and I asked them how many people saved in the crusade ended up in local

churches. Not one person who gave his heart to Christ in that crusade ended up in the local church.

These statistics of an 84 to 97 percent fall-away rate are not confined to crusades but are typical throughout local church evangelism. Nor is this strictly a U.S. phenomenon. Missionaries confirm that the statistics are the same in South America and Europe. An evangelist with a well-known international evangelism ministry noted a similar problem in their overseas efforts:

> Many came to Christ, but when I started to do follow-up with them, I discovered they understood the Gospel as a self-advancing thing and when I explained it more accurately to them, most walked away from it. God loving them was fine. God wanting a good life for them was fine. Their being sinful and Jesus being the only way, well, that was not acceptable. We fail them if we are not clear on those two things.

These statistics of an 84 to 97 percent fall-away rate are not confined to crusades but are typical throughout local church evangelism.

I could not agree more with his last statement. The problem is not with crusades, but with the methods and message of modern evangelism.

"Following Up" Stillborns

A respected minister, whose evangelism program has exploded across the world, said that his evangelism course attempts to get at the heart of the fall-away rate of new converts "by placing great stress on the follow-up." However, "following up" with a false convert is like putting a stillborn baby into intensive care. Neither approach solves the problem.

Sometimes there is confusion between "follow-up" (meaning "we need to follow the new converts around because they will 'fall away' if we don't") and discipleship (meaning "teaching them to observe all things that I have commanded you," Matthew 28:20). I believe in feeding converts; I believe in nurturing them. Discipleship is biblical and most necessary. But I don't believe in following them. I can't find it in Scripture.

Consider the Ethiopian eunuch. Not only was the new convert immediately left without follow-up, he was returning to an entirely un-Christian nation. How could he survive? *All he had was God and the Scriptures.* This is because his salvation was not dependent on Philip, but on his relationship with the indwelling Lord.

Follow-up is when we get decisions, either through crusades or the local church, and we take laborers from the harvest field, who are few as it is, and give them the disheartening task of running after these "converts" to make sure they are continuing with God. This is a sad admission of the amount of confidence we have in the power of our message and in the keeping power of God. In light of the fact that God "is able to keep you from falling, and to present you faultless before the presence of his glory with exceeding joy" (Jude 1:24, KJV), either He is not able to keep converts, or His hand is not in their profession of faith in the first place. If He has begun a good work in them, He will complete it until that day (Philippians 1:6). If He is the author of their faith, He will be the finisher of their faith (Hebrews 12:2). He is able to save to the uttermost those who come to God through Him (Hebrews 7:25). Jesus said, "No one will pluck you from My Father's hand" (John 10:29).

It is encouraging when a true conversion takes place because there will be little need for any "follow-up." More than likely you will hardly be able to keep up with the convert yourself, as he puts his hand to the plow and does not look back (Luke 9:62). When I passed from death to life way back in 1972, I immediately began devouring God's Word, I disciplined myself to pray, I shared my faith with all who would listen, and I didn't need to be coaxed into fellowship. I wanted to be with other Christians. I think that is a normal, biblical conversion.

I am not the only one who believes that the problem is not a lack of follow-up. Jim Elliff, President of Christian Communicators Worldwide, writes:

> A great mistake is made by blaming the problem on poor follow-up. In many churches there is every intention and effort given to follow-up, yet still the poor numbers persist. One church followed up "by the book," seeking to disciple people who had been told they were new converts during the crusade of an internationally-known evangelist. The report of the pastor in charge was that none of them wanted to talk about how to grow as a Christian. He said, "In fact, they ran from us!"... [Churches] have learned to accept the fact that people who profess to have become Christians often have to be talked into going further, and that many, if not most, simply will not bother. Authentic new believers can *always* be followed up, however, because they have the Spirit by which they cry, "Abba Father" (Rom. 8:15). They have been given love for the brethren, and essential love for the beauty

and authority of the Word of God. But you *cannot* follow-up on a spiritually dead person. Being dead, he has no interest in growth.[44] (emphasis in original)

The problem is that Lazarus is four days dead (see John chapter 11). We can run into the tomb, pull him out, prop him up, and open his eyes, but "he stinketh" (v. 39). He needs to hear the voice of the Son of God.

The sinner is dead in his sins. We can say, "Pray this prayer," but he needs to hear the voice of the Son of God, or there is no life in him; and the thing that primes the sinner's ear to hear the voice of the Son of God is the Law. It is the Law that converts the soul, so that the person becomes a new creation in Christ (see 2 Corinthians 5:17).

A well-known preacher of the past had warned, "Evermore the Law must prepare the way for the gospel. To overlook this in instructing souls is almost certain to result in false hope, the introduction of a false standard of Christian experience, and to fill the Church with false converts...Time will make this plain."

If we continue to disregard the importance of using the Law in bringing people to salvation, we will continue to witness the devastating results revealed in this chapter. When we speak about the hundreds of thousands who fall away from the faith, we can lose sight of the reality that these are individual human beings, and at stake is their eternal salvation from death and damnation. We simply must stop telling people under God's wrath and headed for Hell that God has a wonderful plan for their lives. If we fear God we will return to the pattern given us in Scripture, to seek and save the lost the way Jesus did. This is what we will examine in the next chapter.

Chapter 7

WHAT DID JESUS DO?

I n recent years it was popular in some sectors of the Church to ask, "What would Jesus do?" And as often happens with catchphrases, it has been taken to extremes —everything from "What would Jesus eat?" to "What would Jesus drive?" At first glance it might seem worthwhile to ask what Jesus would do in a particular circumstance, but the question has an inherent flaw: it opens the door to speculation. The answer becomes open-ended so that people can make up whatever "Jesus" they want to fit anything they would like to do: "What would Jesus do? I'll tell you what He *wouldn't* do. He wouldn't condemn people because they want an abortion, and He wouldn't go around ramming religion down people's throats!"

The better question to ask is, "What *did* Jesus do?" This confines our answers to the safe and reliable boundaries of the Bible.

What did Jesus do when He confronted sinners? As we have seen from Scripture, He made the issue one of righteousness rather than happiness. Jesus said that unless our *righteousness* exceeds that of the scribes and Pharisees, we would not enter the kingdom of Heaven (Matthew 5:20). He told us to seek first the kingdom of God and His *righteousness* (Matthew 6:33), and assured us that those who hunger and thirst for *righteousness* will be filled (Matthew 5:6). It is the Law that makes us thirst after a *righteousness* that we have no desire for.

Before I was a Christian, I had as much desire for righteousness as a four-year-old boy has for the word "bath." The Bible says, "There is none who seeks after God" (Romans 3:11). It says that men love the darkness and hate the light, and they will not come to the light lest their deeds be exposed (John 3:19,20). The only thing they drink in is iniquity like water (Job 15:16). But the night I was confronted with the spiritual nature of God's Law and understood that God requires truth in the inward parts (Psalm 51:6), that He saw my thought life and considered lust to be the same as adultery and hatred the same as murder, I began to see that I was condemned and asked, "What must I do to be made *right?*" I began to thirst for righteousness. The Law put salt on my tongue. It was a schoolmaster to bring me to Christ.

Law to the Proud, Grace to the Humble

Earlier we looked at the fact that Jesus came to preach the gospel, the Good News, to those who were *spiritually* poor, who were brokenhearted *over their sin*, etc. (see Luke 4:18,19). This is because God looks on the one who "is poor and of a contrite spirit, and who trembles at [His] word" (Isaiah 66:2). The gospel of grace is not for the proud, but for the humble. Only the sick need a physician, and only those who are convinced of the disease will appreciate and appropriate the cure.

Therefore, biblical evangelism is always, without exception, Law to the proud and grace to the humble. Never once did the Son of God give the Good News (the cross, grace, and mercy) to a proud, arrogant, or self-righteous person. Why? Because He always did those things that please the Father. God *resists the proud* and gives grace to the humble (James 4:6; 1 Peter 5:5). "Everyone who is proud of heart," Scripture says, "is an abomination to the Lord" (Proverbs 16:5). Only after the Law has been used to humble a person is he then ready for the message of grace. As Charles Spurgeon stated, "They must be slain by the law before they can be made alive by the gospel."

A. W. Pink said:

> Just as the world was not ready for the New Testament before it received the Old, just as the Jews were not prepared for the ministry of Christ until John the Baptist had gone before Him with his claimant call to repentance, so the unsaved are in no condition today for the Gospel till the Law be applied to their hearts, for "by the Law is the knowledge of sin." It is a waste of time to sow seed on ground which has never been ploughed or spaded! To present the vicarious sacrifice of Christ to those whose dominant passion is to take fill of sin, is to give that which is holy to the dogs.

What did Jesus mean when He said not to give what is holy to the dogs? To what was He referring when He said not to cast pearls before swine, lest they trample them under their feet, and turn and tear you in pieces (Matthew 7:6)? The most precious pearl the Church has is "Christ crucified." Preach grace to the proud and watch what they do with it. They will trample the blood of the Savior under their feet with their false profession, and, what is more, they will become enemies of the gospel. If not physically, they will surely tear you in pieces verbally.

Those who make a profession of faith without having a humble heart (which the Law produces) have the experience described in 2 Peter 2:22: "According to the true proverb: 'A dog returns to his own vomit,' and 'a sow, having washed, to her wallowing in the mire.'" This is the tragic result of casting pearls of the gospel of grace to the proud, or what the Bible calls "dogs" and "swine."

The false convert has never "crucified the flesh with its passions and desires" (Galatians 5:24). He, like the pig, must go back to wallowing in the mire. Pigs need to wallow in mire because they crave the slime to cool their flesh. So it is with the false convert. He never repented, so his flesh is not dead with Christ. It is instead burning with unlawful desire. The heat of lust is too much for his sinful heart; he must go back to the filth.

To avoid the tragedy of false conversions, we must follow the principle of using the Law to break the hard heart and the gospel to heal the broken heart. So let's look briefly at biblical examples of giving the Law to the proud and grace to the humble.

In Luke 10:25–37 we read that a certain lawyer stood up and tested Jesus. This is not an attorney, but a professing expert on God's Law. He asked Jesus, "Teacher, what shall I do to inherit eternal life?" Now, what did Jesus do? He gave him the Law. Why? Because the man was proud, arrogant, self-righteous. The spirit of his question was, "And what do *You* think we have to do to get everlasting life?" So Jesus asked him, "What is written in the law? What is your reading of it?" The man said, "'You shall love the LORD your God with all your heart, with all your soul, with all your strength, and with all your mind,' and 'your neighbor as yourself.'" Jesus replied, "Do this and live."

Then Scripture says, "But he, *wanting to justify himself*, said to Jesus, 'And who is my neighbor?'" The Living Bible brings out more clearly the effect of the Law on the man: "The man wanted to justify (his lack of love for some kinds of people), so he asked, 'Which neighbors?'" While he did not mind Jews, he disliked Samaritans. So Jesus then told him the story of what we call the "good Samaritan" who was not "good" at all. In loving his neighbor as much as he loved himself, the Samaritan merely obeyed the basic requirements of God's Law. And the spirituality of the Law (what the Law demands in truth) had the effect of stopping the lawyer's mouth. He did not love his neighbor to that degree. The Law was given to stop every mouth and leave the whole world guilty before God.

Similarly, in Mark 10:17–22, a rich, young ruler came running to Jesus, knelt before Him, and asked, "Good Teacher, what shall I do that I may inherit eternal life?" It would seem that his earnest and humble heart made him a prime candidate as a potential convert. How would most of us react if someone came up and asked, "How can I get everlasting life?" We'd say, "Oh, quickly, say this prayer before you change your mind." But what did Jesus do with His potential convert? He didn't give him the message of God's grace. He didn't even mention the love of God. Neither did He tell him of an abundant, wonderful new life. Instead, Jesus first corrected his understanding of "good," saying that only God was good. He then used God's standard of goodness—the Moral Law—to expose the man's hidden sin. Jesus gave him five horizontal Commandments, those having to do with his fellow man. When the man claimed to have kept them, revealing his self-righteousness, Jesus said, "One thing you lack," and He used the essence of the First Commandment ("I am the LORD your God...You shall have no other gods before me," Exodus 20:2,3) to show the man that he was a transgressor. God was not foremost in his life. The rich young man loved his money, and one cannot serve both God and money. The Law brought him the knowledge of sin. Then the Scriptures reveal that it was *love* that motivated Jesus to speak in this way to this rich, young ruler (see v. 21).

Every time we witness to someone, we should examine our motives. Do we love the sinner enough to make sure his conversion is genuine?

Every time we witness to someone, we should examine our motives. Do we love the sinner enough to make sure his conversion is genuine? If Jesus had accepted at face value the young man's profession of righteousness, He might have led him into a false conversion. Instead, Jesus gave the Law to this proud, self-righteous man.

Then we see grace being given to the humble in the case of Nicodemus (John 3:1–21). Nicodemus was a leader of the Jews, whom Jesus called a "teacher of Israel" (v. 10). He was therefore thoroughly versed in God's Law. He also had a humble heart, because he came to Jesus and acknowledged the deity of the Son of God (v. 2). So Jesus gave this sincere seeker of truth the Good News of the penalty being paid: "For God so loved the world that He gave His only begotten Son." And it was not foolishness to Nicodemus but the "power of God to salvation."

Think of the woman caught in the very act of violating the Seventh Commandment. She was condemned by the Law for adultery. She had no excuse—her guilty mouth was stopped (see Romans 3:19)—and a merciless Law called for her blood. It brought her trembling to Jesus, where she found mercy. Or consider Zacchaeus, a Jew whose words reveal he knew the demands of the Law. His actions also reveal that he had a humble heart. No doubt there weren't many proud Pharisees climbing trees to see Jesus. A knowledge of sin via the Law caused him to thirst for righteousness and humbly seek after the Savior. His willingness to pay restitution to any he had defrauded shows that his heart was prepared for grace.

Peter likewise used the principle of Law to the proud and grace to the humble. On the Day of Pentecost, his audience was composed of "devout men" who were gathered to celebrate the giving of God's Law on Mount Sinai. Peter told these Jews that they were "lawless"—that they had violated God's Law by murdering Jesus (Acts 2:23). He drove home that fact by saying, "Therefore let all the house of Israel know assuredly that God has made this Jesus, whom *you crucified*, both Lord and Christ" (v. 36). It was then that they realized their sin was personal. They were "cut to the heart" and cried out for help. Only after the Law convicted them of their sinfulness did Peter offer them grace (v. 38).

The apostle Paul also followed the principle of Law before grace. After warning that God will judge humanity by the Moral Law (Romans 2:12), he tells his hearers that the work of the Law is written on the human heart, and that it concurs with the conscience (v. 15). Then he begins to use the Law evangelistically, personalizing each Commandment to his self-righteous hearers:

> You, therefore, who teach another, do you not teach yourself? You who preach that a man should not steal,

do you steal [Eighth Commandment]? You who say, "Do not commit adultery," do you commit adultery [Seventh Commandment]? You who abhor idols, do you rob temples [Second Commandment]? You who make your boast in the Law, do you dishonor God through breaking the Law? For "The name of God is blasphemed [Third Commandment] among the Gentiles because of you," as it is written. (vv. 21–24)

Paul used the Law to bring the knowledge of sin. He also said, "Imitate me, just as I also imitate Christ" (1 Corinthians 11:1). So make sure you follow Paul's example of how to witness biblically, because he was merely following the way of the Master. As Charles Spurgeon stated, "Only by imitating the spirit and the manner of the Lord Jesus shall we become wise to win souls."

The Way of the Master

I am a strong believer in following in the footsteps of Jesus. I would never approach someone and say, "Jesus loves you." It is totally unbiblical; there is no precedent for it in Scripture. Neither would I begin by saying, "I'd like to talk to you about Jesus Christ." Rather, we need to bring the knowledge of the disease of sin (using the Law) *before* we offer the cure of the gospel.

In John chapter 4, we can see an example of personal witness as Jesus speaks to the Samaritan woman at the well. He started in the natural realm (talking about natural water), then transitioned to the spiritual (mentioning "living water"), brought conviction using the essence of the Seventh Commandment, then revealed Himself as the Messiah. So, when I approach someone, I may talk about the weather, sports, or some current topic to get to know them for a couple of minutes, maybe joking lightheartedly, and then I deliberately swing from the natural to the spiritual. I do this by using gospel tracts. (We sell millions of unique tracts that are appealing to the unsaved—they often even ask for more![45])

I may say, "Did you get one of these? It's a gospel tract. What do you think happens when someone dies—do you think there's an afterlife?" Whatever he answers, I say, "If there is a Heaven, do you think you are good enough to go there?"

Almost everyone thinks they are headed for Heaven because they are morally good. Proverbs 20:6 even tells us that: "Most men will proclaim each his own goodness." This is because they do not have a true definition of "good." Romans 7:12 tells us that the Law is good, so I do what Jesus did with the rich, young ruler who did not understand what "good" meant, and what Paul did in Romans chapter 2. I take him through the Ten Commandments to show him God's definition of good:

"How many lies do you think you have told?"

"Oh, I've lost count."

"What does that make you?"

"I guess that would make me a liar."

People are not offended by such an approach because you are just asking them questions about their favorite topic—themselves.

"Have you ever stolen anything, regardless of the value?"

"No."

I'll sometimes say with a smile, "Come on, you've just admitted to me that you're a liar. Have you ever stolen anything in your life, even if it's small?"

He says, "Yes, when I was young."

"What does that make you?"

"A thief."

"Jesus said, 'Whoever looks at a woman to lust for her has already committed adultery with her in his heart.' Have you ever done that?"

"Yeah, plenty of times."

"Have you ever used God's name in vain?"

"Yeah, I've been trying to stop."

"Do you know what you're doing? Instead of using a four-letter filth word to express disgust, you're using the name of the God who gave you life. That's called blasphemy, and the Bible says, 'The LORD will not hold him guiltless who takes His name in vain' [Exodus 20:7].

"I'm not judging you, but *by your own admission*, you're a lying, thieving, blasphemous, adulterer at heart, and you have to face God on Judgment Day. And we've only looked at four of the Ten Commandments."

Because the Law is written on his heart (see Romans 2:15), the man's conscience accuses him—acknowledging the truth of what I am saying—and the Law condemns him. I then ask, "So if God judges you by this standard on the Day of Judgment, will you be innocent or guilty?"

"Guilty."

"Do you think you will go to Heaven or Hell?"

And the usual answer is, "Heaven"—probably a result of the modern gospel. So I ask, "Is that because you think God is good and He'll overlook your sins?"

He says, "Yeah, that's it. He'll overlook my sins."

"Imagine saying that in a court of law. Let's say you've committed rape, murder, drug pushing—very serious crimes. The judge says, 'You're guilty. All the evidence is here. Have you anything to say before I pass sentence?' And you say, 'Yes, judge. I believe you are a good man and you will overlook my crimes.' The judge would probably say,

'You are right about one thing. I *am* a good man, and *because* of that, I am going to see that justice is done. *Because* of my goodness, I am going to see that you are punished for your crimes.' And the thing that sinners are hoping will save them on the Day of Judgment—the goodness of God—will be the very thing that will condemn them. Because if God is good, He must by nature punish murderers, rapists, thieves, liars, fornicators, and blasphemers. God is going to punish sin wherever it is found."

So with this knowledge, the man is now able to understand. He has been given light that his sin is primarily vertical, that he has "sinned against heaven" (Luke 15:21). He realizes that he has angered a holy God by violating His Moral Law and that the wrath of God abides on him (John 3:36). He can see that he is "weighed in the balance" of eternal justice and "found wanting" (Daniel 5:27), so that he now understands the need for a sacrifice.

The thing that sinners are hoping will save them on the Day of Judgment—the goodness of God—will be the very thing that will condemn them.

He is therefore ready for the Good News, and can now comprehend the incredible love of God in Jesus Christ: "Christ has redeemed us from the curse of the law, having become a curse for us" (Galatians 3:13). "God demonstrates His own love toward us, in that while we were still sinners, Christ died for us" (Romans 5:8). We broke the Law, and Jesus paid our fine. That means God can legally dismiss our case. It's as simple as that.

When you use the Law to show sinners their true state, be prepared for them to thank you. For the first time in their lives, they will see the Christian message as expressing love and concern for their eternal welfare rather than merely proselytizing for a better lifestyle while on this earth. They will begin to understand why they should be concerned about their eternal salvation. The Law shows them that they are condemned by God. It even makes them a little fearful—and "the fear of the Lord is the beginning of wisdom" (Psalm 111:10; Proverbs 9:10).

Early in 2010, I was preaching open-air at Huntington Beach to about eighty people. A man had been heckling me when his wife called out, "I have given up on God. I was a Catholic and I had eight miscarriages!"

I asked how many living children she had, and said, "Have you thanked God for your two healthy children? Have you thanked Him for your eyes? You can see; you're not blind. Have you thanked Him for your brain? You can think. Have you thanked Him for this wonderful free country into which you were born, and for your handsome husband?"

When she boldly said, "I thank *science* for my children," I replied, "It's *God* who opens the womb, not science. Do you think you are a good person?"

"I'm a *very* good person."

"How many lies have you told in your life? Have you ever stolen something, irrespective of its value?" etc.

She admitted having had lied and stolen, so I spoke of Judgment Day, the reality of Hell, the fact that even though we are guilty criminals and that God is a righteous Judge, Jesus stepped in and paid our fine for us. Because of the death and resurrection of the Savior, God can legally dismiss our case—He can commute our death sentence upon our repentance and faith in Jesus.

After I had finished preaching, the man and his wife sought me out and gratefully accepted some literature. They were not offended, and even asked for my email address. I did not ask for a decision from either of them. I simply left them in the hands of a faithful Creator, knowing that it is the gospel that is the power of God to salvation.

Take the same approach with a Mormon, a Muslim, an intellectual—anyone to whom you want to witness. Most Christians think that they have to bury their heads in the Koran or the Book of Mormon before they can witness effectively to those groups. Not so. Just bury your head in the Bible. God's Word is sufficient. When you lift up your head you should have your mind filled with truths such as these: "I would not have known sin except through the law" (Romans 7:7); "Now we know that whatever the law says, it says to those who are under the law, that every mouth may be stopped, and all the world may become guilty before God" (Romans 3:19); "The law was our schoolmaster to bring us to Christ" (Galatians 3:24, KJV); and "The law of the LORD is perfect, converting the soul" (Psalm 19:7).

The biblical gospel message is applicable to all people everywhere—whether they are happy or hurting, rich or poor, in the U.S. or overseas, in a high-rise or a lowly hut, regardless of their beliefs or their lifestyles. While we must be culturally sensitive, we do not need to tailor specific outreaches to each individual group because the disease of sin and the cure of the Savior apply to all humanity. God has given light to every man, and the universal Moral Law is written on the heart of all people in all cultures.

Must we use the Law every time we witness? No. Just keep in mind the biblical principle of Law to the proud, and grace to the humble. If the person is proud or self-righteous, he needs the Law to humble him. You can determine pride by what comes out of his mouth. Simply ask, "Do you think you are a good person?" (Most individuals think they deserve to go to Heaven because they are good.) If he says that he is, then you need to do what Jesus did in Mark 10:17,18—take him through the Commandments to show him that he is not morally good, and that he needs the Savior. If he is humble of heart, has a biblical understanding of the nature of sin, and is genuinely contrite, he needs the gospel (but people like this are very few and far between).

Nor do we need to concern ourselves with the idea that we should befriend sinners and address their "felt needs" before speaking to them about salvation. It may take weeks, months, or even years before we get around to talking to them about the subject of sin. On the other hand, if we understand sin in its true light as enmity with God (see Romans 8:7) and we grasp the urgency of the situation—that our unregenerate friend could die tonight and face God's righteous judgment—would we not be motivated to show our friend her depravity in relationship to the Law, and to use the Law to appeal to her conscience in order to bring her to repentance and salvation?

Let's see how a "felt needs" approach would work in a court of law with a child molester. Take for instance the man who kidnapped a seven-year-old girl from her Southern California home in 2002. He sexually molested her, strangled her to death, set her little body on fire and left her in the desert. Imagine the judge saying the following during this man's trial: "All the evidence is in. You are guilty. However, I don't want to deal with your guilt at the moment. I want to first address your felt needs. Are you happy? Do you have an emptiness inside?"

Such talk would be absurd. Any judge who asked such things would be thrown off the bench. The criminal is in court because he has committed a serious offense, and that is the *only* subject that should be addressed. Justice must be served. The man must be punished for his terrible crime. His felt needs have nothing to do with the issue.

After studying Scripture, you should also know that the area of battle is not the sinner's intellect but his conscience. So if you just want to argue, stay in the intellect; but if you want sinners to surrender to Jesus Christ, move the battle into the conscience, using the Law of God to bring the knowledge of sin. That is what I did with the woman at Huntington Beach. I could have spent time arguing with her about whether science or God had given her two healthy children, but I instead asked her if she thought she was a good person, addressing her conscience. This is because the conscience is the God-given ally right in the heart of enemy territory. It bears witness with the Commandments, convincing sinners to drop their defenses and surrender all.

Charles Spurgeon said regarding the importance of the "weapon" of the Law:

> Lower the Law and you dim the light by which man perceives his guilt; this is a very serious loss to the sinner rather than a gain; for it lessens the likelihood of his conviction and conversion. I say you have deprived the gospel of *its ablest auxiliary [most powerful weapon]* when you have set aside the Law. You have taken away from it the schoolmaster that is to bring men to Christ . . . They will never accept grace

till they tremble before a just and holy Law. Therefore the Law serves a most necessary purpose, and it must not be removed from its place.

I am so thankful to God for giving us such an incredible weapon in our battle for the lost. I so concur with John Wesley when he said of the Law, "Yea, love and value it for the sake of Him from whom it came, and of Him to whom it leads. Let it be thy glory and joy, next to the cross of Christ. Declare its praise, and make it honorable before all men."

Some criticize the title of our television program, "The Way of the Master," believing it is a little presumptuous of us to put Jesus "in a box" and say that He evangelized a certain way. However, He is our example. J. C. Ryle reminds us of the importance of following in His steps:

> People will never set their faces decidedly towards heaven, and live like pilgrims, until they really feel that they are in danger of hell...Let us expound and beat out the Ten Commandments, and show the length, and breadth, and depth, and height of their requirements. This is the way of our Lord in the Sermon on the Mount. We cannot do better than follow His plan.
>
> We may depend on it, men will never come to Jesus, and stay with Jesus, and live for Jesus, unless they really know why they are to come, and what is their need. Those whom the Spirit draws to Jesus are those whom the Spirit has convinced of sin. Without a thorough conviction of sin, men may seem to come to Jesus and follow Him for a season, but they will soon fall away and return to the world.

Chapter 8

RAIDERS OF THE CONTENTS OF THE LOST ARK

P roverbs 6:23 tells us that the "commandment is a lamp, and the law a light." In 1980, when the Ten Commandments were removed from the schools of the United States, it left a generation in the dark as to moral absolutes. We now live at a time when a breed of human beings can kill, steal, hate, dishonor their parents, and revile God without qualms of conscience.

Today's generation doesn't just lack the moral values of its grandparents; it doesn't have *any* moral values. In previous years, there was a "moral" code even among criminals, that when you stole from someone, you didn't blast him with your gun as you left. This is not so nowadays. We are daily reminded that what one generation permits the next embraces as normality. Years ago, a woman would hesitate to walk in front of a group of men out of concern that they would undress her with their eyes. These days, her fear is that she will be viciously raped, sodomized, and murdered.

In light of the statistics we considered in the beginning of this book, it would seem that the enemy has removed from the Body of Christ its ability to be salt and light in a dark and decaying world. Jesus warned that if salt lost its flavor, it would be good for nothing except to be trampled underfoot by men. This is why so many hold the Church in contempt. The world has trampled us underfoot, and is reaping terrible consequences.

We are living in times of gross darkness, but remember, this is not a "God-forsaken" world—it is a world that has forsaken God. He can, in His great sovereignty, open Satan's clenched fist and drop the riches of revival into the lap of the Church. Eric W. Hayden, in his book *Spurgeon on Revival*, wrote, "Almost every book dealing with spiritual awakening or a revival of history begins by describing the pre-revival situation in approximately the same words. For instance, you will read such words as these: 'The darkness before the dawn'; 'The sleep of midnight and gross darkness'; or 'dissolution and decay.' W. T. Stead, who was a child of the Welsh Revival of 1859, when writing of the later revival in the twentieth century, said of it: 'Note how invariably the revival is preceded by a period of corruption.'"

While the Church was asleep, the enemy did this. It is now time for followers of Christ to awaken out of our stupor and get back to biblical evangelism.

There is great hope for the masses of false converts who sit within the Church. It is a rich field of evangelistic endeavor. The fact that they are still there reveals that they remain open to the things of God. History shows us that virtually every major revival of the past has been birthed out of a great awakening of those who thought they were saved, but were not. I have seen this teaching awaken many false converts to their true state. God has soundly saved them, and they have begun to be the witnesses they are commanded to be.

Enemy Attack

How did this problem arise in the Church in the first place? How was it that so many tares have been sown among the wheat? In Matthew 13:25, Jesus tells us why it happened and who was behind it: "But while men slept, his enemy came and sowed tares among the wheat, and went his way." While the Church was asleep, the enemy did this. It is now time for followers of Christ to awaken out of our stupor and get back to biblical evangelism.

When speaking of using the Law as a schoolmaster to bring sinners to Christ, Martin Luther said, "This now is the Christian teaching and preaching, which God be praised, we know and possess, and it is not necessary at present to develop it further, but only to offer the admonition that it be maintained in Christendom with all diligence. *For Satan has attacked it hard and strong from the beginning until present, and gladly would he completely extinguish it and tread it underfoot.*" Luther also stated, "Satan, the god of all dissension, stirreth up daily new sects, and last of all (which, of all other, I should never have foreseen or once suspected), he hath raised up a sect of such as teach…that men should not be terrified by the Law, but gently exhorted by the preaching of the grace of Christ."

In addition to sowing tares among the wheat, Satan duped the Church into believing that it is advancing by getting decisions for Christ without use of the Law. We are in a very real war with a very real enemy who has invaded our ranks and stripped the gospel of its power. The ark has been raided.

Remember that in the Old Testament, the ark of the covenant signified God's presence. It was not the ark that God prized; it was what the ark contained. Have you ever wondered why God manifested Himself in such a glorious way that the priests in the house of the Lord could not minister (1 Kings 8:10,11)? It happened when the priests brought in the ark of the covenant. Scripture tells what the ark contained:

> There was nothing in the ark except the two tablets of stone which Moses put there at Horeb. (v. 9)

It seems God so esteems His Law that He could not withhold His glorious presence from the temple. The psalmist didn't say, "Oh, how I love Your *ark!*" Paul didn't say, "I delight in the *ark* of God." It was God's holy Law that they loved and revered. That Law was written with the finger of God and is an expression of His holy, perfect character. We, as individuals and as the Church, are the "temple of the Lord," and when we give the Moral Law its rightful place, perhaps we will truly see the power of His presence—something that causes demons to tremble.

Satan hates this teaching for a number of reasons. It awakens false converts to their true state. It puts the fear of God into the heart of Christians, helping them to walk in holiness. It gives them great motivation to reach out to the lost, knowing that the issue is not merely the happiness of sinners in this life, but their eternal welfare in the light of a wrath-filled Creator.

As Luther said, the enemy has attacked the use of the Law in evangelism "hard and strong from the beginning until present." However, our great consolation is the fact that this is *God's* teaching, and I believe that it is His timing to bring it to light. The Law magnifies grace and opens sinners' eyes to the gospel so that the cross makes sense—and isn't that our greatest desire, for God to be glorified and sinners saved from Hell? We want to see genuine worldwide revival, so that the "earth will be filled with the knowledge of the glory of the LORD, as the waters cover the sea" (Habakkuk 2:14).

It was A. W. Pink who said, "It is true that [many] are praying for worldwide revival. But it would be more timely, and more scriptural, for prayer to be made to the Lord of the Harvest, that He would raise up and thrust forth laborers who would fearlessly and faithfully preach those truths which are calculated to bring about a revival." I firmly believe that the use of the Law in evangelism is one of those truths, and if we want to see a great harvest of souls in these last days, we must hold onto this truth with unwavering conviction.

Free from Their Blood

If you experience a problem with muscle pain, a well-meaning physician might prescribe the FDA-approved drug Lyrica. Before you take it, however, consider these possible side effects: swelling of the face, mouth, lips, gums, tongue, or neck; trouble breathing; rash, hives, or blisters; swelling of hands, legs, and feet; dizziness; sleepiness; blurry vision; weight gain; trouble concentrating; dry mouth; feeling "high"; depression; and suicidal thoughts or actions (attempting or committing suicide).[46] Sometimes the "cure" is worse than the disease.

The "wonderful plan" message promises a cure to the world's ailments, and millions have gladly swallowed its message unaware of its terrible side-effects, in this life and in the next. Think of what that message has produced: those who say they know the Lord but kill their children in the womb; who think that Jesus sinned; who do not believe in a real enemy; who regularly lie, steal, fornicate, and have lustful thoughts. Think of the multitude who will cry, "Lord, Lord," and hear the horrific words, "I never knew you." Then there is the added side-effect of those we erroneously call "backsliders" (who never slid forward in the first place), who fall away from the faith and face a latter end worse than the beginning.

May the following letter, written by a pastor, stir your heart to do all that you can to avoid leading anyone into a false conversion:

Dear Brother Ray,

I have been a pastor for 25 years. I always thought I was doing a reasonably good job. Kind of like the folks who consider themselves "good people." I had tried to preach, what I thought, was the whole counsel of God. I prayed, over the years, with many people to accept Jesus and make Him Lord of their lives.

My wife, Judy, and I moved to Ruidoso, New Mexico, about six years ago to plant a church. Shortly after arriving I was convicted that something was horribly wrong with my ministry. I read the Scriptures and prayed earnestly that God would show me what was wrong. The feeling continued to grow and I became depressed and moody. I asked Judy to pray for me and explained my problem. I didn't know if this was the Holy Spirit convicting or Satan attacking. She prayed that God would reveal the cause of my depression and make Himself clear as He revealed any problem with my ministry for Him.

That night I had the most terrifying, realistic, blood-chilling nightmare any man has ever had. I am a Vietnam veteran and I know a little about nightmares. Nothing in my experience has ever come close, nor do I ever want it to, to the horror of that night!

I dreamed that it was Judgment Day and I was standing right next to the throne of God. I noticed that to my left and my right were pastors as far as I could see. I thought this was odd that the Lord would reserve this front-row space for pastors only.

I looked out across a space of only a few yards and there were millions, maybe billions, of people, yet I could see each one of their eyes staring at me. As I studied this group I noticed that I knew many of them from times at the altar or ones who had sat under my teaching. I was pleased to see that they had made it to heaven, but confused because they didn't look happy. They looked very angry and hateful.

Then I heard the voice of the Lord say, "Away, I never knew you." I was suddenly frightened that what I was seeing were those who *thought* they were saved. Then I saw all of them pointing a finger at each of us pastors and saying together, in one voice that shook my soul, *"We sat in your church and thought we were saved. Why didn't you tell us we were lost?"*

Tears were pouring down my face and the faces of all of those pastors. I watched as one by one those people were cast into hell. One and then another, and another, and another..., until they were all gone. I died inside as each one screamed in agony and gnashed their teeth, cursing us as they went into the lake of fire.

Then I was looking into the face of Jesus and He said to me, "Is this the part where I'm supposed to say, 'Well done, my good and faithful servant'?" I woke up with a scream and my heart pounding and I was begging Jesus to forgive me.

I died a million deaths that night. Since that night I have done two things on a daily basis. I do everything I can to preach the Law before grace in the hope that conviction of sin will bring a sinner to true salvation. The other thing that I do is pray for every person I have ever preached to, asking God to repair any damage I have done. I also never believe anyone when they tell me they are saved. It is my duty to challenge them and search out the solidness of their salvation.

Your ministry and material have been a great blessing to me. I am learning to be more effective and confident as I teach others how to share their faith by using the Law. I have seen several people saved, who thought they were saved, as I have used the "Way of the Master" material to teach them evangelism.

I do want to hear those words, "Well done, my good and faithful servant," and thanks to you and your team I have a better chance of hearing them. Thank you! I just wanted to let you know, some pastors are waking up to the truth. The desire of my heart is to please God. I pray that my days of being a man-pleaser are over along with the nightmares. I also pray that God will use me to bring other pastors into the truth of the Gospel message so that they will not have to face the nightmare that I did.

Steve Kreins
First Church of God, Waco, Texas

Since the Fall of man, there has been a great battle for the souls of men and women. Those who have gone before us in past centuries have not had an easy task. But they knew if they followed according to the pattern of God's Word, with His help, they would eventually deliver sinners from death and Hell. If they sowed in tears, they would reap in joy. They wanted, above all things, to be "true and faithful witnesses." If they preached the whole counsel of God, they would be innocent of the blood of all men (see Acts 20:26,27). These ministries, of men such as Wesley, Wycliffe, Whitefield, Spurgeon, and many others, were greatly effective in reaching the lost. The key was in the careful and thorough use of the Law to prepare the way for the gospel. We are wise to follow in their footsteps.

Some point to Paul's statement "that I might by all means save some" and say, "We are not confined to using the Law to reach the lost. We can use any and *all* means to reach the unsaved." But note the context of Paul's words:

> To the Jews I became as a Jew, that I might win Jews; to those who are under the law, as under the law, that I might win those who are under the law; to those who are without law, as without law (not being without law toward God, but under law toward Christ), that I might win those who are without law; to the weak I became as weak, that I might win the weak. I have become all things to all men, that I might by all means save some. (1 Corinthians 9:19–22)

Paul was saying (as one preacher put it) that when he saw a Jew, he hid his ham sandwich behind his back. The New Living Translation states it this way: "I try to find common ground with everyone, doing everything I can to save some." His "all means" is in the context of godly congeniality, for the sake of the sinner's salvation—not a license to use any and every (unbiblical) means to reach the lost.

If you have questions about respected ministries that have preached the modern gospel, may I respectfully suggest that you do what the Bereans did with Paul's teaching —and what I did when I first discovered these principles. Search the Scriptures daily to see if these things are so (see Acts 17:11). *Please* do that, for the sake of eternal souls. If the principles mentioned in this book are indeed biblical, then drop every manmade method and reach the lost according to the God-given pattern.

If you are a pastor, you have a unique and wonderful calling. You are to "preach Christ, warning every man...., that [you] may present every man perfect in Christ Jesus" (Colossians 1:28). You have been entrusted with the eternal souls of precious human beings. In Hebrews 13:17, Scripture speaks of that trust and of its fearful accountability, telling the flock that leaders "watch out for your souls, as those who must give account. Let them do so with joy and not with grief." Imagine the unspeakable grief of standing before Almighty God and hearing members of your flock saying, "But my pastor never warned me!" Imagine hearing them cry "Lord, Lord!" and seeing them cast out of Heaven into Hell. Forever.

The size of our churches mean nothing if they prove to be full of false converts. May each of us give an account with joy, and not with grief.

Thank you for being open-minded and allowing me to share my heart with you. May God continue to bless you and grant you your heart's deepest desires, as you delight yourself in Him.

FOR MY CAMPUS CRUSADE FRIENDS

Over the years that I have shared my concerns about contemporary evangelism, I have been careful never to name names. However, many have rightly guessed that on occasion I have been referring to the widely used tract "The Four Spiritual Laws," penned by Dr. Bill Bright, co-founder of Campus Crusade for Christ. With approximately 2.5 billion copies distributed in all major languages of the world, the tract has been very instrumental in popularizing the modern gospel presentation.

I have enjoyed breakfast with the current President of Campus Crusade for Christ (CCC), Steve Douglass, and count him as a friend and brother in Christ. I especially enjoyed being interviewed by him on his program, and I consider it an honor to do anything with CCC. Steve is a wonderful man of God who has a deep passion for the lost. So let me assure those who think our ministries are at odds that there is no animosity.

However, some ardent supporters of CCC believe that the "Four Spiritual Laws" approach is the only correct way to witness, and have strongly objected to the use of the Ten Commandments in evangelism. Any who would honestly examine Dr. Bright's writings, especially those toward the end of his life, would find that they *are not opposed* to the principles in this book. In fact, his writings are consistent with what I have been saying.

In July 2002, Kirk and I were invited to Orlando, Florida, to join Dr. Bright at his home for breakfast. After our meal, we sat down in his living room and heard this warm, humble, sincere man of God (then in his eighty-first year) share his heart with us. Let me use his own words from his book *Heaven or Hell*, released that same month, to convey the essence of what he said to us (in all the following excerpts, the emphasis is mine):

> In His approximately 42 months of public ministry, there are 33 recorded instances of Jesus speaking about hell. No doubt He warned of hell thousands of times. The Bible refers to hell a total of 167 times.
>
> I wonder with what frequency this eternal subject is found in today's pulpits. *I confess I have failed in my ministry to declare the reality of hell as often as I have the love of God and the benefits of a personal relationship with Christ.* But Jesus spent more of His time warning His listeners of the impending judgment of hell than speaking of the joys of heaven.
>
> ...I have never felt the need to focus on telling people about hell. However, as a result of a steady decline in morals and spiritual vitality in today's culture and a growing indifference to the afterlife, I have come to realize the need for a greater discussion of hell...I have thus come to see that *silence, or even benign neglect on these subjects, is disobedience on my part.* To be silent on the eternal destinations of souls is to be like a sentry failing to warn his fellow soldiers of impending attack. It is like knowing calamity is coming and not sounding the alarm.[47]

By admitting that "benign neglect on these subjects is disobedience on my part," Dr. Bright revealed his honest humility and his genuine love of the truth. He also humbly acknowledged that, by emphasizing God's love and the benefits of coming to Christ, his approach was not in keeping with Jesus' teaching.

In *Red Sky in the Morning* (published in 1998), after lamenting the rampant hypocrisy among professing believers, Dr. Bright identifies reasons for the problems in the Church. Among the reasons he cites are the fact that many who call themselves Christians really are not (they are false converts); that many have ignored vital biblical truths about worldliness, sin, and judgment; and that "the pure gospel is not being preached." Instead, pastors "tread lightly past the fundamentals, handing out a sugar-coated version of faith to men and women whose souls are in eternal jeopardy."[48] He also admits, "We have misrepresented the Christian life," explaining:

> *Many preachers mention only the benefits of the Christian life without addressing the necessary disciplines, the trials, and temptations we will endure.* With our culture's emphasis on owning earthly possessions and living the good life, these pastors are fearful of acknowledging the biblical facts about the testing the apostles experienced for their faith. Should we expect anything less in our own lives? The Bible tells us clearly that all believers will undergo difficulties, trials, and tests.
>
> *A belief that Christians are entitled to the "good life" can result in demoralized church members.* Expecting the Christian life to be a bed of roses can be very discouraging to new believers—and to more mature

ones as well—when they are jostled by the storms of life. (pp. 217–218)

In the same book, he earnestly pleads with Christians to clean up their lives, then concludes the publication with two pages devoted to the Ten Commandments.

The Significance of the Law

Near the end of his life, he devoted an entire book to explaining the significance of God's Law for both believers and unbelievers. The following passages, from *Written by the Hand of God* (published in 2001),[49] reveal his understanding of the Law's purpose:

> The Ten Commandments are sometimes called the Decalogue. They have God as their Author, holiness as their theme, and *the exposure of ungodly hearts as their purpose*. Consider the powerful reality of ten statements carved in stone, 5,000 years old, and still *cutting hearts to the quick*. They go where no glib tongue nor guileful technology can travel to *show us all how desperately wicked we are*. (p. 35)

> Just read through the Ten Commandments, and without a moment's hesitation, you will concede you have failed to live up to God's perfect standards... *When I think about my failure to live according to God's perfect Law, I am driven to the truth of the cross of Jesus Christ* and His incredible work of salvation on my behalf. I am reminded of my own sinfulness and what a worm I am in the sight of a holy and just God. (p. 40)

> When I see my reflection in the holy Law of God, I see a picture of *a man in need of grace*. (p. 43)

The great 19th century preacher Charles Spurgeon remarked of the Law's purpose, "*The Law is meant to lead the sinner to faith in Christ, by showing the* impossibility of any other way. It is the black dog to fetch the sheep to the shepherd, the burning heat which drives the traveler to the shadow of the great rock in a weary land."... *Apart from the deadening effect of the Law, no one would feel the need to cast himself at the mercy of Christ.* (pp. 47–48)

What motivated this woman to return to her husband? It was *the transforming power of God's Word, His Law, in her heart. The more she saw herself in the mirror of God's Word, the more she was driven to her knees in need of God's grace...* (p. 56)

Since the time of Moses, the *Ten Commandments have shown people their sin and hopelessness and their need for the grace of God in Christ Jesus.* Again, God never meant the Ten Commandments to act as a means of earning salvation. Rather, *God's Law provides a way for people to see their total inadequacy to live by God's standards.*

...Paul writes, "No one can ever be made right in God's sight by doing what His law commands. For *the more we know God's law, the clearer it becomes that we aren't obeying it*" (Romans 3:20). *Our failure shows us our need for grace.*

It is *amazing how powerful God's timeless principles are when it comes to revealing our sin* and shortcomings. One old story tells of a smalltown newspaper editor in west Texas who had some space to fill so he had the Ten Commandments set in type and ran them in the paper without comment. Seven men left town the next day and another wrote, "Cancel my subscription. You're getting too personal."

... This is the real significance of the Ten Commandments. *Because they reveal God's perfect holiness, we see ourselves as God sees us—in need of His grace and forgiveness.* (pp. 58–59)

Who is God's grace for? It is for sinners... It also says that *anyone who sins breaks the Law of God: "Those who sin are opposed to the law of God, for all sin opposes the law of God"* (1 John 3:4). The cost of sin is death. (p. 59)

But today the relationship between the Ten Commandments and God's grace has often been presented in a misleading way. Like two heavyweight fighters sparring off against one another in the ring, Law and grace have been presented as two old warriors battling for our hearts and minds. But the fact is *Law and grace are absolutely, beautifully intertwined.* (p. 60)

When God gave the world the Law, He gave us His transcendent standard. It goes beyond what we can see, hear, feel, or smell. It is a standard untouched by human hands. God's Laws do not bend or shift depending on the era in which we live, the circumstances in which we find ourselves, or the environment in which we were raised. The Ten Commandments were given to the ancient Hebrews as *a beacon to the world, a standard for everyone to know what God expects* in relation to Him and others. (p. 64)

But if disobeyed, *the Ten Commandments become the standard God uses to judge our lives.* (p. 254)

As these passages demonstrate, Dr. Bright clearly recognized the biblical role of the Law in evangelism, to bring the knowledge of sin and lead sinners to the Savior.

A God of Love

Some consider the use of the Ten Commandments to be counter to the traditional CCC approach of beginning with God's love, but as Dr. Bright himself writes about the "Four Spiritual Laws" tract in *Witnessing Without Fear*, "We don't claim that it's the only way to share the gospel, or even the best way; but it is one method that works."[50] Among the benefits he lists is that "it begins on a positive note: 'God loves you.'"[51]

Regarding a focus on God's love, recall that in *Heaven or Hell*, written the year before his death, Dr. Bright acknowledges that an overemphasis on God's love and an underemphasis on impending judgment and Hell has had a negative result. In the same book he explains:

> Although God is loving and merciful, He is also holy, righteous, and just. To emphasize some of His attributes at the expense of others creates a distorted view of who God is and therefore creates false expectations of what He will do at the judgment seat. (p. 35)

This is in keeping with his earlier comments in *GOD: Discover His Character* (1999),[52] in which he explains the importance of having an accurate view of God. He writes:

> If we exalt one of God's qualities over another, we can get a distorted view of God's character. In fact, overemphasizing any one of God's attributes to the exclusion of others can lead to heresy. For example,

teaching only about God's mercy and neglecting His role as a judge will prevent people from understanding God's hatred of sin and the future punishment for wrongdoing. (p. 36)

In other words, by presenting God only as loving—and neglecting to mention that He also is just and will judge all sin—we present a distorted view of God and prevent people from seeing their need for a Savior. In *GOD: Discover His Character*, Dr. Bright extols the various attributes of God—not just His love, but His holiness, justice, and wrath, among others:

> *God gives laws* and promises *that establish His nature as one of holiness and integrity.* If the people obeyed these laws, they would be blessed and happy; *if they did not, they would bring God's wrath and judgment upon themselves.* (p. 25)

> God's holiness demands consequences for sin. *We have broken His standard of holiness, and His holiness demands that He judge sin*, not ignore or excuse it. (p. 133)

> Over and over again, *we set up our own standards of what ought to please God:* "I deal fairly with people." "I do not abuse my wife or my children." "I give to the needs of others in the homeless ministry I support." "I'm a good neighbor."
> ...*None of our manmade standards of behavior meet the requirements of a holy God.* God's holiness mandates that we keep all His laws perfectly at all times. (pp. 134–135)

> God's spiritual laws are no less binding [than His physical laws]. As the perfect Judge and Lawgiver,

God is also the law enforcer. *His laws lay out the responsibilities for which God holds us accountable.* They are a yardstick by which God measures our righteousness. When His laws are broken, *He must punish anyone who defies His righteous laws.* (p. 175)

As the holy and righteous sovereign of the universe, God cannot ignore or overlook any act of sin. David writes, "God is a judge who is perfectly fair. *He is angry with the wicked every day.*"

God's anger over sin should never be underestimated: "You spread out our sins before You—our secret sins—and You see them all. We live our lives beneath Your wrath...Who can comprehend the power of Your anger? *Your wrath is as awesome as the fear You deserve.*" (p. 194)

God predicts judgment for the ungodly: "It is mine to avenge; I will repay. In due time their foot will slip; their *day of disaster* is near and their *doom* rushes upon them." Yet many live as though they will never be judged. They scoff at the idea of an *eternal hell.*

The final judgment has, however, been part of the biblical message for thousands of years. The Holy Spirit inspired Paul to write this ominous warning:

> Because of your stubbornness and your unrepentant heart, *you are storing up wrath against yourself for the day of God's wrath*, when His righteous judgment will be revealed. God "will give to each person according to what he has done." To those who by persistence in doing good seek glory, honor and immortality, He will give eternal life. But for those who are self-seeking and who reject the truth

and follow evil, *there will be wrath and anger.*
(pp. 196–197)

What Do We Tell Sinners?

In the above passages, Dr. Bright acknowledges that man tends to create his own standards of goodness; therefore he needs to see himself in light of God's holy standard. All who violate God's Law rightly incur His anger and wrath and will suffer the terrible consequences on Judgment Day. A "day of disaster," "doom," and "eternal hell" are not what people would consider a "wonderful plan," and Dr. Bright doesn't propose that we tell sinners of God's love for them. Rather, in these pages he urges us to "warn" them of the coming judgment and call them to repentance:

> Does a friend or family member need to be told that God is a God of justice?... *Lovingly warn someone* who has not acted justly that God judges those who do wrong. (p. 198)

> The time is so urgent to *call people to repentance.* We do not know who has a tomorrow, or whose hearts are soft toward God...While we ourselves must be ready, *we must warn those who have not heard of His gracious mercy* or who have not heeded God's call. (pp. 238–239)

In the same book, Dr. Bright mentions that he reviews and meditates on the Ten Commandments each day, encouraging readers to do the same. He then leaves readers with this admonition:

> I urge you to begin right now through prayer and witnessing to *help others know and apply the righteous standards of our loving God.* (p. 187)

He obviously does not object to the use of the Ten Commandments in witnessing, since he affirms their importance and recommends their use.

In *Heaven or Hell,* Dr. Bright likewise identifies the Ten Commandments as the God-given standard by which we recognize our sin and the need for grace:

> As I read the Bible, I read of a God of love and compassion...But I also read of a God who is holy. Therefore, *He has provided us with His Ten Commandments* (Exodus 20:3–17) and the Golden Rule (Matthew 7:12) *to establish a standard of holiness for our lives.*
>
> *In the Ten Commandments, we can clearly understand our sinfulness and our need for His grace.* [He then takes the time to use the Law lawfully, by quoting every one of the Ten Commandments.]
>
> How many of these have you broken? The Bible says that to offend God in breaking one of these is to have broken all of them! The truth is that everyone has broken God's perfect Law. We have each lied, or looked at a person lustfully, or coveted someone else's property. Who, then, can stand before a holy God?
>
> Because God is holy, He cannot, will not, allow sin in His presence...Because He is also just, He cannot let sin go unpunished. *Breaking these commandments will take us to hell without the intervening grace and mercy of Jesus Christ.* (pp. 35–37)

He again emphasizes our responsibility, not to tell the lost about God's love, but to *warn* them of the dangers of an eternal Hell:

> It is the duty of every believer to *warn others of the reality of hell*...Our world cannot afford to be lied to about such a crucial issue as hell. Every believer

must see this present hour as a God-sent opportunity to *warn the lost of the dangers of hell*. (pp. 43–44)

G. Campbell Morgan, a 19th century preacher of renown, said, "I am bound to admit that I have seen *a far larger number surrender to Christ when I have been preaching on the terrible results of neglecting salvation* than when dwelling on any other theme."

And J. C. Ryle added, "The watchman who keeps silent when he sees a fire is guilty of gross neglect. The doctor who tells us we are getting well when we are dying is a false friend, and *the minister who keeps back hell from his people in his sermons is neither a faithful nor a charitable man*."

Therefore, we should be like the prophet Ezekiel, the "watchman on the wall," telling our society, family, friends, and neighbors of the reality of heaven and hell. We are to be engaged in "snatching them from the flames of judgment" (Jude 23). This act simply requires *caring enough to warn of the very real danger* of living without Christ. *We need only tell people the truth: There is a hell to shun and a heaven to gain.* We must join the apostle Paul who declared, "It is because we know this solemn fear of the Lord that we work so hard to persuade others" (2 Corinthians 5:11). It is our duty to share eternal truths with those we encounter. (pp. 44–45)

I could not agree more with his heartfelt admonition.

Confirming the Use of the Law

If you feel at all threatened or angered by what I am saying in this book, you need not. The preceding excerpts show that the use of the Ten Commandments in witnessing is not something that Dr. Bright would have felt was heretical.

In fact, Dr. Bright's staff reviewed an earlier edition of this book extolling the use of the Law, titled *Revival's Golden Key*, and vouched for the soundness and value of its message. When it was approved for offering to pastors at Dr. Bright's Beyond All Limits conference in 2002, the reviewer expressed that he "would like to see that everyone gets a copy," and stated, "Hopefully, this message will spread and take hold of many lives." In recent years, the CCC leadership has offered several of our resources in mailings to their donors.

CCC has also trusted me to write for their magazine (*Worldwide Challenge*), I have spoken for them a number of times, and in 2005 the radio program "Women Today with Vonette Bright" even featured the Ten Commandments in a witnessing scenario and pointed listeners to our web site. Following is a transcript:

> Jeff had a real burden to share Jesus! And he did it in one of the toughest areas of town. One man he encountered had not only a hard look in his eyes, but tattoos everywhere. And he'd been in prison much of his life. Most of us would've walked in the opposite direction. But not Jeff. He boldly asked the man, "Have you ever broken the Ten Commandments?" To Jeff's surprise, the man wept. Jeff proceeded to tell him that Jesus came to die for his sins. The man was amazed that anyone would do that for him. Right there on the streets of one of the most dangerous areas of that city—Jeff led his new brother to the Lord. There may be someone you'll encounter today who needs Christ! Share the good news of the gospel. Inspired by Way of the Master, www.way-ofthemaster.com.

In 2008 and 2009, I was privileged to be invited to record five programs for CCC's "Lighthouse Report," which is hosted by Steve Douglass, the President of Campus Crusade for Christ. Steve told me personally that he had listened to and loved "Hell's Best Kept Secret" (my primary message on the use of the Law, the essence of which is contained in this book).

In one program, Steve prompts me to tell how I shared the gospel with "Ed." Ed thought he was headed for Heaven because he's a good person, so I took him through a few of the Ten Commandments. Since he admitted to being guilty of breaking them, I explained what God did for him so he wouldn't have to go to Hell, then encouraged him to repent and trust in Jesus. Ed replied, "Hey, thanks for talking to me. This has been good!" In a friendly encounter that took only a couple of minutes, Ed was made aware of his sin and his need for the Savior, and he was not at all offended by this approach. Neither was Steve. He encourages listeners at the end: "So, why don't you try that approach this week?"

The Heart of the Matter

I am certain that the desire of Dr. Bright's heart, and his goal for the CCC ministry, was not to promote the "Four Spiritual Laws" tract in and of itself. Rather, his desire was to fulfill the Great Commission. Remember, Dr. Bright himself said that the tract is *not* the "only way to share the gospel, or even the best way." Those who believe the "Four Spiritual Laws" tract should be used exclusively would benefit from a careful reading of Dr. Bright's later writings.

As the excerpts in this appendix clearly show, Dr. Bright emphasized the power of the Ten Commandments to reveal our true state before God, bring the knowledge of sin, make sin appear exceedingly sinful, convict the conscience, magnify the grace of God, and serve as a schoolmaster to lead sinners to Christ. He noted that the Law is God's unchanging standard by which He will judge all mankind—one that transcends time, place, and circumstances, making it suitable for sharing with the people at the World Trade Center on September 10. And he encouraged its use in evangelism. He also addressed the importance of conveying an accurate view of God's character, cautioning readers not to overemphasize His love while ignoring His holiness, justice, wrath, etc. All of these are biblical principles mentioned throughout this book.

In *Witnessing Without Fear*, Dr. Bright suggests "a careful reading of the New Testament" to determine the method of evangelism "modeled for us throughout Scripture."[53] Please, for the sake of the lost, follow Dr. Bright's advice: examine Scripture to see what Jesus, the disciples, and the early Church did.[54]

Be sure you don't just speak about God's love, but also warn the lost about His wrath against sin, the coming Day of Judgment, and the reality of Hell. As Dr. Bright himself confessed, to be silent on these subjects was "disobedience on my part." So to avoid being guilty of "benign neglect," make sure you follow the biblical principles he cited.

If you use the "Four Spiritual Laws" approach, simply make four important changes:

1) Be careful not to misrepresent the Christian life by telling sinners that Jesus will improve their lives with a wonderful plan. Don't be like the many preachers who, as Dr. Bright noted, wrongly *"mention only the benefits of the Christian life without addressing the necessary disciplines, the trials, and temptations we will endure."*

2) Avoid the unbiblical mistake of giving the cure of the gospel before you've convinced of the disease of sin. Dr. Bright rightly stated, *"Apart from the deadening effect of the Law, no one would feel the need to cast himself at the mercy of Christ."*

3) Take the time to open up the Ten Commandments to bring the knowledge of sin and lead sinners to Christ. *"Since the time of Moses,"* Dr. Bright wrote, *"the Ten Commandments have shown people their sin and hopelessness and their need for the grace of God in Christ Jesus."*

4) Remember to put in what has been left out. Faithfully include the terrible realities of Judgment Day and Hell. Keep in mind Dr. Bright's admonition: *"Every believer must see this present hour as a God-sent opportunity to warn the lost of the dangers of hell."*

Most of us tend to look down at the Pharisees with a sense of scorn. It is hard to understand how anyone could prefer their own religious traditions to the Word of the Living God. But if you and I understand the biblical legitimacy of the use of the Law to reach the lost, yet ignore it and instead preach the traditional modern message, we are no better than them.

However, it is my sincere hope that you see what is at stake, and that you do not prefer the traditions of men above the Word of God. I trust that you are being as the Bereans, and that you are testing what this book has said by the standard of the Scriptures ... and that you will "hold fast what is good" (1 Thessalonians 5:21).

ENDNOTES

1. Adrienne S. Gaines, "Nearly 1 Million Make Decisions for Christ in 'Great Awakening' Tour," May 15, 2009 <www.charismamag.com/index.php/news/20728>.
2. "Exciting World Missions Statistics," Epimeno, July 4, 2009 <www.emmausministries.org/epimeno/?cat=14>.
3. Eric Young, "CCC Media Ministry Records Over 10M Decisions in 2009," *The Christian Post*, December 18, 2009 <www.christianpost.com/article/20091218/ccc-media-ministry-records-over-10m-decisions-in-2009/index.html>.
4. Christ for All Nations <https://secure2.cfan.org/UKGB_Impact Newsletter.aspx>.
5. Barna Group, "Morality Continues to Decay," November 3, 2003 <www.barna.org/barna-update/article/5-barna-update/129-morality-continues-to-decay>.
6. Rachel K. Jones, *et al.*, "Patterns in the Socioeconomic Characteristics of Women Obtaining Abortions in 2000–2001," Perspectives on Sexual and Reproductive Health, September/October 2002, 34(5):226–235.
7. Mark Bergin, "Porn Again," *World Magazine*, April 23, 2005 <www.worldmag.com/articles/10555>.
8. Ibid.
9. Barna Group, "Christianity Is No Longer Americans' Default Faith," January 12, 2009 <www.barna.org/barna-update/article/12-faithspirituality/15-christianity-is-no-longer-americans-default-faith>.
10. Barna Group, "Most American Christians Do Not Believe that Satan or the Holy Spirit Exist," April 10, 2009 <www.barna.org/barna-update/article/12-faithspirituality/260-most-american-christians-do-not-believe-that-satan-or-the-holy-spirit-exis>.
11. Barna Group, "Barna Survey Examines Changes in Worldview Among Christians over the Past 13 Years," March 6, 2009 <www.barna.org/barna-update/article/21-transformation/252-barna-survey-examines-changes-in-worldview-among-christians-over-the-past-13-years>.
12. Ibid.
13. Barry A. Kosmin and Ariela Kaysar, American Religious Identification Survey 2008 <www.americanreligionsurvey-aris.org/reports/ARIS_Report_2008.pdf> (Table 1).
14. George Barna, *Real Teens: A Contemporary Snapshot of Youth Culture* (Ventura, CA: Regal Books, 2001), pp. 126–128.
15. "Joint Call to Incite a Cross-Culture Revolution," March 10, 2003 <www.charitywire.com/charity31/03467.html>.

16. Barna Group, "Fewer Than 1 in 10 Teenagers Believe that Music Piracy is Morally Wrong," April 26, 2004 <www.barna.org/barna-update/article/ 5-barna-update/139-fewer-than-1-in-10-teenagers-believe-that-music-piracy-is-morally-wrong>.

17. "Joint Call."

18. Jon Walker, "Family Life Council says it's time to bring family back to life," SBC.net, June 12, 2002 <www.sbcannualmeeting.net/sbc02/news-room/newspage.asp?ID=261>.

19. This trend, and its solution, is addressed in my book *How to Bring Your Children to Christ... & Keep Them There* (Genesis Publishing Group).

20. James A. Smith Sr., "Researcher offers 'modest proposal' for increasing baptisms," *Baptist Press*, May 4, 2005 <www.sbcbaptistpress.org/ bpnews.asp?id=20724>.

21. Founders Ministries Blog <www.founders.org/blog/2005/08/does-conversion-make-difference.html>.

22. Mary Fairchild, "Christianity Today: General Statistics and Facts of Christianity" <www.christianity.about.com/od/denominations/p/ christiantoday.htm>.

23. For a thorough biblical survey of the evangelistic approach used by Jesus and the disciples, see *What Did Jesus Do?* (Genesis Publishing Group).

24. Associated Press, "Colorado Church Gunman Had Grudge Against Christian Group, Cops Say," December 10, 2007 <www.foxnews.com/ story/0,2933,316322,00.html>.

25. World Health Organization, "Cancer" <www.who.int/cancer/en/>.

26. World Health Organization, "The top 10 causes of death" <www.who.int/mediacentre/factsheets/fs310/en/index.html>.

27. World Health Organization, "Pedestrians, cyclists among main road traffic crash victims" <www.who.int/mediacentre/news/releases/2009/ road_safety_report_20090615/en/index.html>.

28. Doug Gross, "Regular flu has killed thousands since January," CNN <www.cnn.com/2009/HEALTH/04/28/regular.flu>.

29. Julie Appleby, "Hospital-acquired infections take toll on bottom lines," *USA Today*, November 21, 2006 <www.usatoday.com/money/indus-tries/health/2006-11-20-infections-usat_x.htm>.

30. Matthew Herper, "Scariest Hospital Risks," *Forbes*, June 14, 2007 <www.forbes.com/2007/06/14/hospital-risk-cdc-ent-manage-cx_ mh_0614riskhospital.html>.

31. Matthew Henry, *Commentary on the Whole Bible, Genesis to Revelation* (Grand Rapids, MI: Zondervan, 1961), p. 1425.

32. Ibid.

33. Hemant Mehta, interviewed by Heather Johnson, "The Atheist Who Went to Church," *Outreach Magazine*, March/April 2007.

34. "A Sure Guide to Happiness," *The Watchtower*, June 15, 2006 <www. watchtower.org/e/20060615/article_02.htm>.

35. Brian White, *Basic Buddhism Guide*, 1993 <www.buddhanet.net/e-learning/5minbud.htm>.

36. Hanrbans Singh, "The Key That Unlocks True Happiness" <www.nirankari.com/literature/utarget/2003/spring_2003/article01.htm>.

37. Maulana Shah Muhammad Abdul Aleem Siddiqui Al Qaderi, "The Quest for True Happiness," World Islamic Mission <www.wimmauritius.org/quest.html>.

38. Joseph Carroll, "Most Americans 'Very Satisfied' With Their Personal Lives," Gallup, December 31, 2007 <www.gallup.com/poll/103483/Most-Americans-Very-Satisfied-Their-Personal-Lives.aspx>.

39. Merle Hertzler, "Is There Happiness Without Jesus?", April 2006 <http://webspace.webring.com/people/xq/questioner/Hope1.htm>.

40. Throughout the book we will be using the term "the Law" to refer to the Moral Law of God or the Ten Commandments. This is consistent with how Jesus referred to "the Law" or "the Law and the prophets" in His teaching (Matthew 5:17; 7:12; 22:40; 23:23; Luke 10:26; 16:16; John 7:19–23). When Paul speaks of "the Law" in Romans 2:20–23 and 13:8,9, he quotes a number of the Ten Commandments, making it clear he is referring to the Moral Law. This is also the case with other writers of Scripture, including James (2:10,11). I have capitalized the Moral Law to differentiate it from civil law.

41. Henry Breeden, *Striking Incidents of Saving Grace* (Hampton, TN: Harvey Christian Publishers, 1981), pp. 188–189.

42. Elmer Murdoch, Step Up to Life <www.stepuptolife.com/Pages/welcome.htm>.

43. Assemblies of God Statistics for 1995–2005 <http://ag.org/discipleship_downloads/AG_Statistics_Charts.pdf>.

44. Jim Elliff, "Southern Baptists, an Unregenerate Denomination," 2005 <www.ccwtoday.org/article_view.asp?article_id=150>.

45. For our collection of gospel tracts, see www.LivingWaters.com.

46. Pfizer website <www.lyrica.com>.

47. Bill Bright, *Heaven or Hell* (Orlando, FL: New*Life* Publications, 2002), pp. 32, 48.

48. Bill Bright and John N. Damoose, *Red Sky in the Morning* (Orlando, FL: New*Life* Publications, 1998), p. 215.

49. Bill Bright, *Written by the Hand of God* (Orlando, FL: New*Life* Publications, 2001).

50. Bill Bright, *Witnessing Without Fear* (Orlando, FL: New*Life* Publications, 2003), p. 66.

51. Ibid, p. 120.

52. Bill Bright, *GOD: Discover His Character* (Orlando, FL: New*Life* Publications, 1999).

53. Bright, *Witnessing Without Fear*, p. 99.

54. See *What Did Jesus Do?* by Ray Comfort (Genesis Publishing Group).

Resources

For additional information on biblical evangelism, please see the following resources.

The Way of the Master: A more thorough, in-depth version of this book, this best-seller teaches you how to share the gospel simply, biblically, and effectively.

What Did Jesus Do? Examine the way that Jesus, the disciples, and great evangelists of the past reached the lost.

The Way of the Master Basic Training Course: This eight-week DVD course (based on the award-winning TV show) is ideal for group training in how to share your faith.

School of Biblical Evangelism: Join more than 10,000 students worldwide—learn to witness and defend the faith in 101 online lessons. Also available in book form.

How to Bring Your Children to Christ...& Keep Them There: Biblical principles to help you guide your children to experience genuine salvation and avoid the pitfall of rebellion.

The Way of the Master for Kids: Answers questions about God, helps children memorize the Ten Commandments and understand why they need Jesus.

Hell's Best Kept Secret / True and False Conversion: Listen to these vital messages free at www.livingwaters.com.

For a complete list of Ray Comfort's resources, conferences, and training Academy, visit www.livingwaters.com.

For **bulk discounts** (as low as $1 per book), please call (800) 437-1893 or see www.livingwaters.com.